ONE + ONE

WRAPS, COWLS & CAPELETS

ONE + ONE

WRAPS, COWLS & CAPELETS

29
PROJECTS FROM JUST TWO SKEINS

IRIS SCHREIER

LARK

An Imprint of Sterling Publishing
387 Park Avenue South
New York, NY 10016

ISBN 978-1-4547-0805-6

Library of Congress Cataloging-in-Publication Data

Schreier, Iris.
 One + one: wraps, cowls & capelets : 29 projects from just two skeins /
Iris Schreier. -- First Edition.
     pages cm
 Includes bibliographical references and index.
 ISBN 978-1-4547-0805-6 (alk. paper)
 1. Knitting--Patterns. I. Title. II. Title: One plus one: wraps, cowls and
capelets.
 TT825.S3928 2014
 746.43'2--dc23
                         2013044511

Distributed in Canada by Sterling Publishing
c/o Canadian Manda Group, 165 Dufferin Street
Toronto, Ontario, Canada M6K 3H6
Distributed in the United Kingdom by GMC Distribution Services
Castle Place, 166 High Street, Lewes, East Sussex, England BN7 1XU
Distributed in Australia by Capricorn Link (Australia) Pty. Ltd.
P.O. Box 704, Windsor, NSW 2756, Australia

For information about custom editions, special sales, and premium and corporate purchases,
please contact Sterling Special Sales at 800-805-5489 or specialsales@sterlingpublishing.com.

Email academic@larkbooks.com for information about desk and examina-
tion copies. The complete policy can be found at larkcrafts.com.

Manufactured in China

2 4 6 8 10 9 7 5 3

larkcrafts.com

contents

CAPELETS

MORE KNITTED ACCESSORIES

introduction

We all end up with orphan skeins that we may not know what to do with. The concept of using two skeins of yarn to complete a garment that began with *One + One: Scarves, Shawls & Shrugs* (Lark, 2012) continues with this third volume of the series. In *One + One: Wraps, Cowls & Capelets*, I'll show you how to combine leftover yarn to create breathtaking capes, wraps, ponchos, scarves, and cowls. The projects range in skill level and techniques, but all of them have one thing in common: They use no more than two beautiful skeins of yarn.

I am honored to present a variety of perspectives here. You'll find designs from a terrific selection of celebrated designers. I also include some of my own designs and some popular knit-along patterns that are unavailable elsewhere.

You'll find patterns suitable for beginner and advanced knitters alike. Some projects, such as the Lace Muse Wrap and the Always the Right Time Striped Shawl, are simple to execute, but the results look more complicated, because the yarn is luxurious and makes the project drape and flow beautifully.

A variety of techniques will ensure that you keep coming back for more time and time again. Here's a sampling: You'll learn how to knit vertically to create a uniquely interesting look with the Egyptian Scarf, or you can master your lace skills with the Elizabethan Collar or the Thick and Thin Wrap. Learn to make a crescent-shaped shawl working side to side and incorporate short rows to angle your work in the Two-Color Sideways Garter Shawl. Use a fabulous slip stitch pattern to create the exquisite Quilted Cowl. Practice colorwork stranded knitting with the Stranded Loop Cowl. Have fun with cables in the Vineyard Shawl. Each piece offers an opportunity to add new skills to your repertoire.

Before you begin, be sure to read through the Techniques chapter beginning on page 120 to get a sense of how some of the techniques and stitch patterns are used. Please use the techniques and patterns in this book as a jumping off point and take liberties to make your own modifications as needed. And be sure to share your project photos with me, either at www.facebook.com/artyarns or through the *One + One: Wraps, Cowls & Capelets* page on www.ravelry.com. Most importantly, enjoy your knitting!

Star Stitch Shoulder Wrap

materials and tools

Artyarns Ensemble Light (50% silk, 50% cashmere; 2.82oz/80g = 400yd/366m): (A), 1 skein, color #922; (B), 1 skein color #1023—approx 800yd/732m of lightweight yarn (3)

Knitting Needles: 4mm (size 6 U.S.) 24"/60cm circular needle, 4.5mm (size 7 U.S.) 24"/60cm circular needle, 5mm (size 8 U.S.) 24"/60cm circular needle or size to obtain gauge

2 split-ring markers

2 buttons, ⅝"/16mm diameter

Tapestry needle

gauge

20 sts = 4"/10cm in Stockinette Stitch on 4mm (size 6 U.S.) needle

14 sts = 4"/10cm in Star Stitch pattern on 4mm (size 6 U.S.) needle

Always take time to check your gauge.

sizes x-small/small (medium/large)

To Fit Bust 28–34 (36–42)"/71–86 (91–107)cm

finished measurements

11½"/29cm tall

55 (65)"/140 (165)cm wide/Upper Edge

66 (74)"/168 (188)cm wide/Lower Edge

The open stitch pattern of this wrap is nice and airy—perfect as a summer piece.

design by
Lynn M. Wilson

skill level
easy

pattern stitches

**STAR STITCH PATTERN
(MULTIPLE OF 3 STS + 5)**

Row 1 (WS): With A, k1, purl to last st, k1.

Row 2 (RS): With B, k3, *yo, k3, pass first of the 3 knit sts over the 2nd and 3rd sts; rep from * ending with k2.

Row 3: With B, k1, purl to last st, k1.

Row 4: With A, k2, *k3, pass first of the 3 knit sts over the 2nd and 3rd sts, yo; rep from * ending with k3.

instructions

With A, beginning at Upper Edge, and 4mm (size 6 U.S.) needle, CO 233 (266) sts.

Next Row: With A, k1, purl to last st, k1.

Work Rows 1–4 of Star Stitch Pattern 5 times.

Change to 4.5mm (size 7 U.S.) needle and work Rows 1–4 of Star Pattern 5 times.

Change to 5mm (size 8 U.S.) needle and work Rows 1–4 of Star Pattern 7 times; then work Row 1 once more.

Next Row: With A, k1, purl to last st, k1.

With A, ending at Lower Edge, loosely bind off all sts.

FINISHING

Along Upper Edge, measure and mark with split ring markers 11½"/29cm and 12"/30cm from one end.

Attach one button at each marker at one end of Wrap. The "holes" or openings nearest the markers on the opposite end are the "button-holes." Weave in ends.

Thick and Thin Wrap

materials and tools

Artyarns Ensemble 4 (50% silk, 50% cashmere; 2.82oz/80g = 200yd/183m): (A), 1 skein, color #909—approx 200yd/183m of medium weight yarn

Artyarns Silk Essence (100% silk; 1.6oz/45g = 400yd/366m): (B) 1 skein, color #909—approx 400 yd/366m of superfine yarn

Knitting needles: 5.5mm (size 9 US) 36"/90cm circular needle or size to obtain gauge.

Tapestry needle

gauge

12 sts/26 rows = 4"/10cm in Stockinette Stitch using A

16 sts/20 rows = 4"/10cm in Stockinette Stitch using B

Always take time to check your gauge.

special abbreviations

Cdd (center double decrease): Slip 2, knit 1, pass slipped stitches over.

Kfb: Knit in front and back of same stitch.

note

This shawl is knitted from the neck down. The first part uses short rows to grow in size, and the second part uses a lace pattern that contains increases.

finished measurements

18 x 82"/46 x 208cm, blocked

This luxurious wrap is so soft and luscious, you'll never want to take it off. The lightness of the lace-weight yarn gives a flouncy free-form flow to the lower body of the shawl. It has a graceful curve that wraps around very easily without falling off.

design by
Iris Schreier

skill level
experienced

instructions

TOP OF SHAWL

With A, CO 4 sts.

Row 1: K1, yo, k2, yo, k1—6 sts.

Row 2: K1, [k1, p1] in yo, p2, [k1, p1] in yo, k1—8 sts.

Row 3: K1, yo, k1, turn; s1, [k1, p1] in yo, k1—10 sts.

Rows 4 and 5: Repeat Row 3—12/14 sts.

Row 6: K1, yo, k to last st, yo, k1—16 sts.

Row 7: K1, [k1, p1] in yo, p1, turn; s1, k2, yo, k1—18 sts.

Rows 8 and 9: Repeat Row 7—20/22 sts.

Row 10: K1, [k1, p1] in yo, p to last 2 sts, [k1, p1] in yo, k1—24 sts.

Rows 11-58: Repeat Rows 3-10 six more times 40/56/72/88/104/120 sts.

Rows 59-67: Repeat Rows 3-9 one time—134 sts.

Row 68: Kfb, [k1, p1] in yo, p to last 2 sts, [k1, p1] in yo, kfb—138 sts.

LACE PANEL (SEE CHART, PAGE 16)

Attach B. Carry A along side. (See Carrying Yarns page 124.)

Row 1: With B, k1, [yo, k8] 17 times, yo, k1—156 sts.

Row 2 and all even rows: K1, p to last st, k1.

Row 3: With B, k1, [yo, k1, yo, ssk, k6] 17 times, yo, k1, yo, k1—175 sts.

Row 5: With B, k1, [yo, k3, yo, ssk, k5] 17 times, yo, k3, yo, k1—194 sts.

Row 7: With B, k1, [yo, k2tog, yo, k1, yo, ssk, yo, ssk, k4] 17 times, yo, k2tog, yo, k1, yo, ssk, yo, k1—213 sts.

Row 9: With B, k1, [yo, k2tog, yo, k3, yo, ssk, yo, k1, cdd, k1] 17 times, yo, k2tog, yo, k3, yo, ssk, yo, k1—215 sts.

Row 11: Switch yarns. With A, k1, [yo, k2tog, yo, k2tog, yo, k1, yo, ssk, yo, ssk, yo, cdd] 17 times, yo, k2tog, yo, k2tog, yo, k1, yo, ssk, yo, ssk, yo, k1—217 sts.

Row 13: With B, k1, [ssk, k7, k2tog, yo, k1, yo] 17 times, ssk, k7, k2tog, k1—215 sts.

Row 15: With B, k1, yo, [ssk, k5, k2tog, yo, k3, yo]17 times, ssk, k5, k2tog, yo, k1—215 sts.

Row 17: With B, k2, yo, [ssk, k3, k2tog, yo, k2tog, yo, k1, yo, ssk, yo] 17 times, ssk, k3, k2tog, yo, k2—215 sts.

Row 19: With B, k1, yo, k2, yo, [ssk, k1, k2tog, yo, k2tog, yo, k3, yo, ssk, yo] 17 times, ssk, k1, k2tog, yo, k2, yo, k1—217 sts.

Row 21: Switch yarns. With A, k1, yo, k4, yo, [cdd, yo, k2tog, yo, k2tog, yo, k1, yo, ssk, yo, ssk, yo] 17 times, cdd, yo, k4, yo, k1—219 sts.

Row 23: With B, k1, yo, k4, k2tog, [yo, k1, yo, ssk, k7, k2tog] 17 times, yo, k1, yo, ssk, k4, yo, k1—221 sts.

Row 25: With B, k1, yo, k4, k2tog, [yo, k3, yo, ssk, k5, k2tog] 17 times, yo, k3, yo, ssk, k4, yo, k1—223 sts.

Row 27: With B, k1, yo, k4, k2tog, [yo, k2tog, yo, k1, yo, ssk, yo, ssk, k3, k2tog] 17 times, yo, k2tog, yo, k1, yo, ssk, yo, ssk, k4, yo, k1—225 sts.

Row 29: With B, k1, yo, k4, k2tog, [yo, k2tog, yo, k3, yo, ssk, yo, ssk, k1, k2tog] 17 times, yo, k2tog, yo, k3, yo, ssk, yo, ssk, k4, yo, k1—227 sts.

Row 31: Switch yarns. With A, k1, yo, k4, k2tog, [yo, k2tog, yo, k2tog, yo, k1, yo, ssk, yo, ssk, yo, cdd] 17 times, yo, k2tog, yo, k2tog, yo, k1, yo, ssk, yo, ssk, k4, yo, k1—229 sts.

Row 33: With B, k1, yo, k3, yo, cdd, yo, [ssk, k3, yo, k1, yo, k3, k2tog, yo, k1, yo] 17 times, ssk, k3, yo, k1, yo, k3, k2tog, yo, cdd, yo, k3, yo, k1—265 sts.

Row 35: With B, k1, yo, k4, yo, cdd, yo, [ssk, k3, yo, k1, yo, k3, k2tog, yo, cdd, yo] 17 times, ssk, k3, yo, k1, yo, k3, k2tog, yo, cdd, yo, k4, yo, k1—267 sts.

Row 37: With B, k1, yo, k5, yo, cdd, yo, [ssk, k3, yo, k1, yo, k3, k2tog, yo, cdd, yo] 17 times, ssk, k3, yo, k1, yo, k3, k2tog, yo, cdd, yo, k5, yo, k1—269 sts.

Row 39: With B, k1, yo, k6, yo, cdd, yo, [ssk, k3, yo, k1, yo, k3, k2tog, yo, cdd, yo] 17 times, ssk, k3, yo, k1, yo, k3, k2tog, yo, cdd, yo, k6, yo, k1—271 sts.

Row 41: With B, k1, yo, k7, yo, k3, yo, [ssk, k3, yo, k1, yo, k3, k2tog, yo, k3, yo] 17 times, ssk, k3, yo, k1, yo, k3, k2tog, yo, k3, yo, k7, yo, k1—311 sts.

Row 43: With B, k9, yo, k2tog, yo, k1, yo, ssk, yo, [ssk, k3, yo, k1, yo, k3, k2tog, yo, k2tog, yo, k1, yo, ssk, yo] 17 times, ssk, k3, yo, k1, yo, k3, k2tog, yo, k2tog, yo, k1, yo, ssk, yo, k9—349 sts.

Row 45: With B, k9, yo, k2tog, yo, k3, yo, ssk, yo, [ssk, k7, k2tog, yo, k2tog, yo, k3, yo, ssk, yo] 17 times, ssk, k7, k2tog, yo, k2tog, yo, k3, yo, ssk, yo, k9—351 sts.

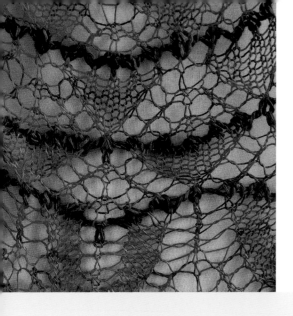

Row 47: With B, k9, yo, k2tog, yo, k2tog, yo, k1, yo, ssk, yo, ssk, yo, [ssk, k5, k2tog, yo, k2tog, yo, k2tog, yo, k1, yo, ssk, yo, ssk, yo] 17 times, ssk, k5, k2tog, yo, k2tog, yo, k2tog, yo, k1, yo, ssk, yo, ssk, yo, k9—353 sts.

Row 49: With B, k9, yo, k2tog, yo, k2tog, yo, k3, yo, ssk, yo, ssk, yo, [ssk, cdd, k2tog, yo, k2tog, yo, k2tog, yo, k3, yo, ssk, yo, ssk, yo] 17 times, ssk, cdd, k2tog, yo, k2tog, yo, k2tog, yo, k3, yo, ssk, yo, ssk, yo, k9—319 sts.

Row 51: Switch yarns. With A, k9, [yo, k2tog] 3 times, yo, k1, [yo, ssk] 3 times, yo, [cdd, yo, k2tog, yo, k2tog, yo, k2tog, yo, k1, yo, ssk, yo, ssk, yo, ssk, yo] 17 times, cdd, [yo, k2tog] 3 times, yo, k1, [yo, ssk] 3 times, yo, k9—321 sts.

Bind off loosely with A. Cut yarn.

FINISHING

Weave in ends.

pattern chart

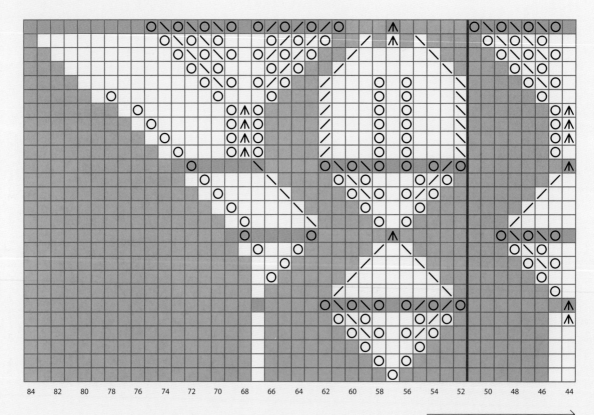

84 82 80 78 76 74 72 70 68 66 64 62 60 58 56 54 52 50 48 46 44

chart continues across page →

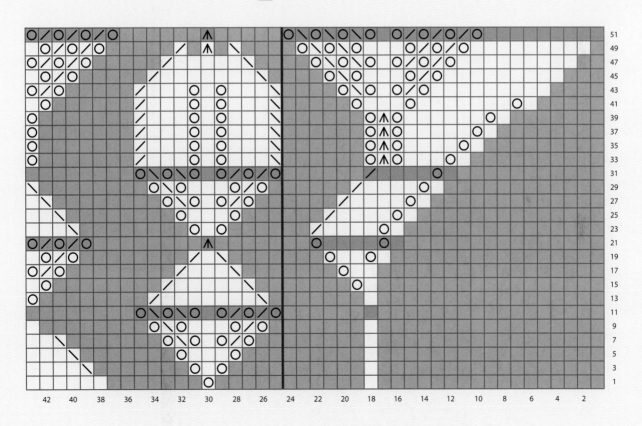

cdd

ssk

k2tog

knit

no stitch

yo

Always the Right Time Striped Shawl

Create stripes at your own discretion with this triangle shawl. Change colors as your heart and mood dictate—there is no right or wrong time. The finished piece is a wonderful accessory to any dressy, business, or casual outfit. It is very soft, light, and warm, and can be a wonderful addition to any travel wardrobe because it can be folded into a small purse without becoming creased.

design by
Judith Rudnick Kane

skill level
beginner

materials and tools

Artyarns Silk Rhapsody Glitter Light (85% silk, 15% kid mohair w/Lurex; 2.82oz/80g = 400yd/366m): (A), I skein, color multi #1020 S; (B), 1 skein, color gray #247 S—approx 800yd/732m of lightweight yarn (3)

Knitting needles: 3.75 mm (size 5 U.S.) 32"/80cm circular needle or size to obtain gauge

Tapestry needle

gauge

20 sts/28 rows = 4"/10cm in Garter Stitch

Always take time to check your gauge.

special abbreviation

Kfb: Knit in front and back of same stitch.

finished measurements

38 x 54"/97 x 137cm

instructions

With A, CO 1 st.

Row 1 (WS): Kfb—2 sts.

Row 2 (RS): Kfb, K1—3 sts.

Row 3: Knit.

Row 4: Kfb, knit to end of row—4 sts.

Row 5: Knit.

Repeat Rows 4 and 5 until there are 190 sts. Bind off loosely. Add 3 strands of 12"/30cm fringe on the edge that has the tails from the color changes. (See page 125 for instructions on adding fringe.) Always remember to increase at the beginning of every right side row. Change colors at your discretion at the beginning of any wrong side row, leaving a 6"/15cm tail to be left as fringe on one edge of the shawl. There is no right or wrong time to change colors. This is art, not science. Relax and enjoy the process.

FINISHING

Weave in ends.

Lace Muse Wrap

materials and tools

Artyarns Cashmere 1-ply (100% cashmere; 1.76oz/50g = 510yd/466m): (A), 1 skein, color marine #107—approx 510yd/466m of superfine yarn

Artyarns Beaded Silk and Sequins Light (100% silk w/ glass beads and sequins; 1.76oz/50g = 110 yd/100m): (B), 1 skein, color #H34S—approx 110yd/100m of lightweight yarn

Knitting needles: 4.5mm (size 7 U.S.) or size to obtain gauge

Stitch markers

Tapestry needle

gauge

27 sts/27 rows = 4"/10 cm in Lace Pattern

Always take time to check your gauge.

notes

1. Wrap is worked in one piece, with 4 garter stitches at each edge when working lace panel sections.

2. Do not cut (A) when changing panels; carry it up along edge when working (B) Garter section. (See Carrying Yarns, page 124.)

finished measurements

14" x 58½"/356cm x 149cm

This glamorous wrap features a simple lace pattern, knit in 1-ply cashmere with sparkly stripes of silk with beads and sequins.

design by
Lisa Hoffman

skill level
intermediate

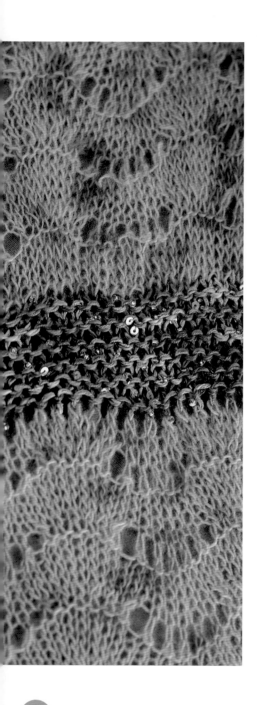

pattern stitches

LACE PATTERN
(MULTIPLES OF 17 STS + 8)

Row 1 (RS): K4, slip marker (sm), knit to last 4 sts, sm, k4.

Rows 2 and 4: K4, sm, purl to marker, sm, k4.

Row 3: Knit, slipping markers.

Row 5: K4, sm, *(k2tog) 3 times, (yo, k1) 5 times, yo, (ssk) 3 times, rep from * to marker, sm, k4.

Row 6: Knit, slipping markers.

instructions

With A, CO 93 sts.

Work 2 rows Garter Stitch (knit each row), setting up markers on first row as follows:

K4, place marker (pm), knit to last 4 sts, pm, k4.

BEGINNING PANEL

Work rows 1–6 of Lace Pattern 4 times and then rows 1–4 once.

MIDDLE PANEL

NOTE: Repeat this panel 5 times.

Change to B, remove markers and decrease on next RS row as follows: *K2tog, rep from * to last st, k1— 47 sts.

Work in Garter stitch for 9 rows, ending having completed a WS row.

Change to A, replace markers and increase on next RS row as follows: *K1, yo, rep from * to last st, k1— 93 sts.

Work rows 2–6 of Lace Pattern once, rows 1–6 six times, and then rows 1–4 once.

END PANEL

Change to B, remove markers and decrease on next RS row as follows: *K2tog, rep from * to last st, k1— 47 sts.

Work in Garter stitch for 9 rows, ending having completed a WS row.

Change to A, replace markers and increase on next RS row as follows: *K1, yo; repeat from * to last st, k1—93 sts.

Work rows 2–6 of Lace Pattern once, rows 1–6 three times, and then rows 1–3 once.

Work 2 rows in Garter Stitch. BO.

FINISHING

Weave in ends. Block by wet block method or steam.

Old and New Shawl

materials and tools

TSCArtyarns Zara Hand-Dyed (100% extrafine merino wool; 3.5oz/100g = 240yd/219m): (A), 1 skein, color #Z16; (B), 1 skein, color #Z23—approx 480yd/438m of lightweight yarn

Knitting needles: 4.5mm (size 7 U.S.) 36"/90cm circular needle or size to obtain gauge

Tapestry needle

gauge

13 sts/24 rows = 4"/10cm in Stockinette Stitch

Always take time to check your gauge.

finished measurements

54"/137cm wide x 9½"/24cm at deepest point

I love combining design elements that are not typically found together in a single project. This shawl has vibrant and modern stripes, with an added edging that is antique and frilly—and unexpected.

design by
Iris Schreier

skill level
easy

● ● ● ○

instructions

With A, CO 3 sts.

Row 1: K1, [yo, k1] twice—5 sts.

Row 2: K1, p to last st, k1.

Row 3: K1, [yo, k1] 3 times—9 sts.

Row 4: K1, p to last st, k1.

Row 5: [K1, yo] 3 times, k to last 3 sts , [yo, k1] 3 times—15 sts.

Row 6: K1, p to last st, k1.

Rows 7 and 8: Repeat Rows 5 and 6—21 sts.

Attach B. Work Rows 9-14 with B.

Row 9: Repeat Row 5—27 sts.

Row 10: K across.

Rows 11-14: Repeat Rows 9-10—39 sts.

Work Rows 15-20 with A: Repeat Rows 5-6—57 sts.

Work Rows 21-26 with B: Repeat Rows 9-10—75 sts.

Work Rows 27-32 with A: Repeat Rows 5-6—93 sts.

Work Rows 33-38 with B: Repeat Rows 9-10—111 sts.

Work Rows 39-44 with A: Repeat Rows 5-6—129 sts.

Work Rows 45-50 with B: Repeat Rows 9-10—147 sts.

Work Rows 51-56 with A: Repeat Rows 5-6—165 sts.

Work Rows 57-62 with B: Repeat Rows 9-10—183 sts. Cut B.

Work Rows 63-64 with A: Repeat Rows 5-6—189 sts.

EDGING

See chart at right.

With A, using Knitted Cast-On, cast on 6 sts.

Rows 1 and 2: K1, ssk, yo2, ssk, yo2, ssk to attach to scarf, turn; sl 1, [k1, p1] into previous row's yo2, k1, [k1, p1] into previous row's yo2, k2.

Rows 3 and 4: K1, ssk, yo2, ssk, yo2, k2, ssk to attach to scarf, turn; sl 1, k2, [k1, p1] into previous row's yo2, k1, [k1, p1] into previous row's yo2, k2.

Rows 5 and 6: K1, ssk, yo2, ssk, yo2, k4, ssk to attach to scarf, turn; sl 1, k4, [k1, p1] into previous row's yo2, k1, [k1, p1] into previous row's yo2, k2.

Rows 7 and 8: Bind off 6 sts, k5, ssk to attach to scarf, turn; sl 1, k5.

Repeat Rows 1-8 46 more times, and bind off remaining sts. Cut yarn.

FINISHING

Weave in ends.

pattern chart

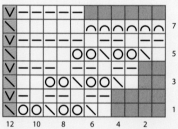

sl st	
▭	purl on RS, knit on WS
OO	yo2
◠	bo
▢	knit on RS, purl on WS
▨	no stitch
◺	ssk

Elena Shawl

materials and tools

Artyarns Ensemble Light (50% silk/50% cashmere; 2.8oz/80g = 400yd/366m): (A), 1 skein, color #2311—approx 400yd/366m of lightweight yarn

Artyarns Ensemble Glitter Light (50% silk/50% cashmere w/Lurex; 2.8oz/80g = 400yd/366m): (B), 1 skein, color #2311S—approx 400yd/366m of lightweight yarn

Knitting needles: 5.5 mm (size 9 U.S.) 24"/60cm circular needle or size to obtain gauge

Tapestry needle

gauge

18 sts/21 rows = 4"/10cm in Stockinette Stitch with one strand of each yarn held together

Always take time to check your gauge.

special abbreviation

Cdd: Slip 2 sts together knitwise, knit 1, pass the slipped sts over the knit st—2 sts decreased

finished measurements

45 x 21"/114 x 53cm, blocked

This shawl is worked from the bottom up. It begins with an adaptation of the Feather and Fan stitch; the eyelet column and the double decrease column are continued through the body of the shawl to the top. This shawl is the perfect size for wrapping loosely around the shoulders while being small enough to be wrapped around the neck like a scarf.

design by
Jennifer Wood

skill level
intermediate

instructions

BOTTOM

NOTE: Use two strands together, one of each color, throughout.

With both yarns held tog, CO 259 sts using the Backward Loop CO. (See Backward-Loop Cast-on, page 122.)

Rows 1-16: Repeat Rows 1-4 of chart 4 times (working section in chart repeat 7 times).

Rows 17-24: Repeat Rows 5-8 of chart 2 times (working section in chart repeat 7 times).

Rows 25-32: Repeat Rows 9-16 of chart 1 time (working section in chart repeat 7 times)—227 sts.

MIDDLE

Next (dec) row (RS): K1, yo, ssk, k11, [Cdd, k11, yo, Cdd, yo, k11] 7 times, Cdd, k11, k2tog, yo, k1—211 sts.

Next Row (WS): K1, purl to last st, k1.

Next Row: Knit.

Next Row: K1, purl to last st, k1.

Next (dec) row (RS): K1, yo, ssk, k10, [Cdd, k10, yo, Cdd, yo, k10] 7 times, Cdd, k10, k2tog, yo, k1— 195 sts.

Next Row (WS): K1, purl to last st, k1.

Next Row: Knit.

Next Row: K1, purl to last st, k1.

Repeat the last 4 rows, working the dec row with 1 less st worked between the Cdd and yo as above, 9 times. There should be 1 st between the Cdd and yo—51 sts.

TOP

1st dec row (RS): K1, yo, ssk, [k3, Cdd, k3, yo, Cdd, yo] 3 times, k3, Cdd, k3, k2tog, yo, k1—43 sts.

Work 3 even rows in pattern as established.

2nd dec row: K1, yo, ssk, [k2, Cdd, k2, yo, Cdd, yo] 3 times, k2, Cdd, k2, k2tog, yo, k1—35 sts.

Work 3 even rows in pattern as established.

pattern chart

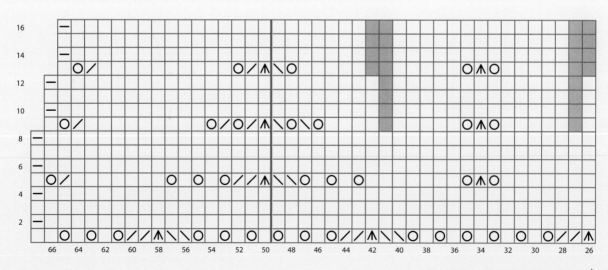

chart continues across page →
(repeats 7 times across)

3rd dec row: K1, yo, ssk, [k1, Cdd, k1, yo, Cdd, yo] 3 times, k1, Cdd, k1, k2tog, yo, k1—27sts.

Work 3 even rows in pattern as established.

4th dec row: K1, yo, ssk, k3, Cdd, k3, yo, Cdd, yo, k3, Cdd, k3, k2tog, yo, k1—23 sts.

Work 3 even rows in pattern as established.

5th dec row: K1, yo, ssk, k2, Cdd, k2, yo, Cdd, yo, k2, Cdd, k2, k2tog, yo, k1—19 sts.

Work 3 even rows in pattern as established.

6th dec row: K1, yo, ssk, k1, Cdd, k1, yo, Cdd, yo, k1, Cdd, k1, k2tog, yo, k1—15 sts.

Next Row (WS): K1, purl to last st, k1.

7th dec row: [Cdd] 5 times—5 sts.

8th dec row (WS): Ssk, p1, k2tog—3 sts.

9th dec row: Cdd—1st.

BO last st.

FINISHING

Weave in ends. Block.

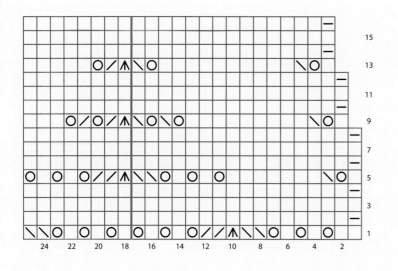

⟍	ssk
⟋	k2tog
☐	knit on RS, purl on WS
Ⓞ	yo
−	knit on WS
⋀	cdd
▨	no stitch

This easy-to-knit triangle shawl is worked from the top down to the bottom edges. Basic garter stitch is alternated with stripes of open elongated stitch while alternating two light and lofty yarns, one with glitter, for texture. The finished shawl is a versatile, reversible piece, large enough to wrap in many ways.

design by
Deborah Frank

skill level
easy

Triangle Lace Shawl

materials and tools

TSCArtyarns TSC Tranquility (60% merino/25% cashmere/15%silk; 2oz/57g = 400yd/366m): (A), 1 skein, color #T22—approx 400yd/366m of lightweight yarn (3)

TSCArtyarns Tranquility Glitter (60% Merino/25% Cashmere/15% Silk with Lurex; 2oz/57g = 400yd/366m): (B), 1 skein, color #TG-22—approx 400yd/366m of lightweight yarn (3)

Knitting needles: 4.5mm (size 7 US) 40"/100cm circular needle or size to obtain gauge

4 stitch markers

1 locking stitch marker or safety pin

Tapestry needle

gauge

20 sts/28 rows = 4"/10cm in Garter Stitch

Always take time to check your gauge.

special abbreviation

KE (Knit Elongated Stitch): Knit 1, wrapping yarn around the needle twice. On the following row, knit the stitch once, dropping the extra wrap from the left-hand needle.

notes

4 stitches are added every RS row (odd-numbered rows). Each 10-row pattern repeat adds 20 stitches to the width of the shawl.

Since the shawl is reversible, it is helpful to place a locking stitch marker on the RS edge of shawl to keep place.

Carry yarn not in use up the side of the work, twisting the working yarn around it.

finished measurements

38½ x 85"/98 x 216cm, blocked

pattern stitches

**TRIANGLE SHAWL
PATTERN REPEAT**

Row 11 (RS): With B, KE2, *sm, yo twice, KE to next marker, yo twice, sm, KE2, repeat from * once more.

Row 12 (WS): Knit each stitch once, dropping extra yarn over from LH needle.

Switch back to A:

Rows 13, 15, 17, and 19 (RS): K2, * slip marker (sm), yo, k to next marker, yo, sm, k2, repeat from *.

Rows 14, 16, 18, and 20 (WS): Knit.

Repeat Rows 11–20 for pattern.

instructions

With A, CO 8 sts.

Knit 2 rows.

SETUP ROWS

Row 1 (RS): K2, place marker (pm), yo, k1, yo, pm, k2 (center sts), pm, yo, k1, yo, pm, k2—12sts.

Rows 2, 4, 6, 8: Knit.

Row 3: K2, sm, yo, k3, yo, sm, k2, sm, yo, k3, yo, sm, k2—16 sts.

Row 5: K2, sm, yo, k5, yo, sm, k2, sm, yo, k5, yo, sm, k2—20 sts.

Row 7: K2, sm, yo, k7, yo, sm, k2, sm, yo, k7, yo, sm, k2—24 sts.

Row 9: K2, sm, yo, k9, yo, sm, k2, sm, yo, k9, yo, sm, k2—28 sts.

Row 10: Knit.

Work Triangle Shawl Pattern. Repeat (Rows 11–20) 14 times—308 sts.

Work Triangle Shawl Pattern. Repeat 2 more times with B only—348 sts.

Next Row (RS): K2, sm, yo, k1, yo, *k2tog, yo * repeat to center marker, sm, k2, sm, *yo, k2tog * repeat until 1 st before last m, yo, k1, yo, sm, k2—352 sts.

Next Row (WS): Knit.

Next Row (RS): Knit.

BINDING OFF

Stretchy Bind-Off (knit loosely):

K1, *k1, sl 2 sts back to LH needle and k2tog tbl, repeat from * across all sts to end. Fasten off.

FINISHING

Weave in ends, leaving 2"/5cm tails to be trimmed after blocking. Submerge shawl in tepid water for about 30 minutes. Do not wring or twist shawl while wet. Remove from water and place it in a dry towel to squeeze excess water out. Lay the shawl on a flat surface and pin out triangle points. Thread wires through yarn over eyelets at top edge and bottom side edges, pinning shawl out to finished measurements. Allow to dry thoroughly before unpinning.

Lacy Silk Coverlet

This coverlet can also be folded and worn as a shawl or a scarf. Its airy lace pattern makes it a standout piece in your wardrobe, and silk yarn gives it a beautiful drape.

design by
Sharon Sorken

skill level
experienced

materials and tools

Artyarns Silk Essence (100% silk; 1.6oz/45g = 400yd/366m): (A), 1 skein, color # H31; (B), 1 skein, color #2269—approx 800 yd/731m of superfine yarn (1)

Knitting needles: 4.5mm (size 7 U.S.) 24"/60cm circular needle or size to obtain gauge, 4.5mm (size 7 U.S.) 10"/26cm straight needles

Waste yarn

Tapestry needle

gauge

20 sts = 4"/10cm in Stockinette Stitch

Always take time to check your gauge.

special abbreviation

St st (stockinette stitch): Knit all right-side rows and purl all wrong side rows.

finished measurements

36 x 36"/91 x 91cm

diamond lace pattern

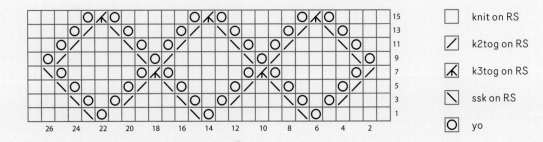

☐	knit on RS
◢	k2tog on RS
◣	k3tog on RS
◥	ssk on RS
Ⓞ	yo

diamond lace border

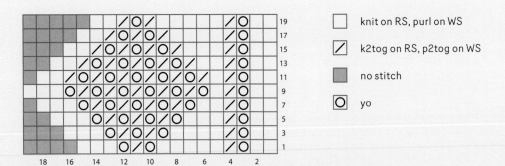

☐	knit on RS, purl on WS
◢	k2tog on RS, p2tog on WS
▨	no stitch
Ⓞ	yo

pattern stitches

DIAMOND LACE PATTERN (MULTIPLE 8 STS + 3)

NOTE: Chart shows odd rows only.

Row 1: K5, yo, *ssk, k6, yo. repeat from * to last 6 sts, ssk, k4.

Row 2 and all even rows: Purl.

Row 3: K3, *k2tog, yo, k1, yo, ssk, k3; repeat from * across.

Row 5: K2, k2tog, yo, k3, yo, ssk, *k1, k2tog, yo, k3, yo, ssk, repeat from * to last 2 sts, k2.

Row 7: K1, k2tog, yo, k5, yo, *k3tog, yo, k5, yo, repeat from * to last 3 sts, ssk, k1.

Row 9: K1, yo, ssk, *k6, yo, ssk, repeat from * to last 8 sts, k5, k2tog, yo, k1.

Row 11: K2, yo, ssk, k3, k2tog, yo,* k1, yo, ssk, k3, k2tog, yo, repeat from * to last 2 sts, k2.

Row 13: *K3, yo, ssk, k1, k2tog, yo, repeat from * to last 3 sts, k3.

Row 15: K4, yo, k3tog, yo, *k5, yo, k3tog, yo, repeat from * to last 4 sts, k4.

Row 16: Purl.

Repeat Rows 1–16 for Diamond Lace Pattern.

DIAMOND LACE BORDER

NOTE: Chart shows odd rows only.

Row 1: (WS) K2, yo, k2tog, k5, yo, k2tog, yo, k3.

Row 2 and all RS rows: K1, yo, k2tog, k to end.

Row 3: K2, yo, k2tog, k4, [yo, k2tog] 2 times, yo, k3.

Row 5: K2, yo, k2tog, k3, [yo, k2tog] 3 times, yo, k3.

Row 7: K2, yo, k2tog, k2, [yo, k2tog] 4 times, yo, k3.

Row 9: K2, yo, k2tog, k1, [yo, k2tog] 5 times, yo, k3.

Row 11: K2, yo, k2tog, k1, k2tog, [yo, k2tog] 5 times, k2.

Row 13: K2, yo, k2tog, k2, k2tog, [yo, k2tog] 4 times, k2.

Row 15: K2, yo, k2tog, k3, k2tog, [yo, k2tog] 3 times, k2.

Row 17: K2, yo, k2tog, k4, k2tog, [yo, k2tog] 2 times, k2.

Row 19: K2, yo, k2tog, k5, k2tog, yo, k2tog, k2.

Row 20: Repeat row 2.

Begin with row 10, repeat rows 1–20, ending with row 9.

DIAMOND LACE BORDER CORNER

Short rows

Row 1: (RS) K1, yo, k2tog, k to last 5 stitches, sl 1, turn, k to end.

Row 2: K1, yo, k2tog, k to last 7 sts, sl 1, turn, k to end.

Row 3: K1, yo, k2tog, k to last 9 sts, sl 1, turn, k to end.

Row 4: K1, yo, k2tog, k to last 11 sts, sl 1, turn, k to end.

Row 5: K1, yo, k2tog, k to last 13 sts, sl 1, turn, k to end.

Rows 6 and 7: K1, yo, k2tog, sl 1, turn, k to end.

Row 8: K1, yo, k2tog, k1, sl 1, turn, k to end.

Row 9: K1, yo, k2tog, k3, sl 1, turn, k to end.

Row 10: K1, yo, k2tog, k5, sl 1, turn, k to end.

Row 11: K1, yo, k2tog, k7, sl 1, turn, k to end.

Row 12: K1, yo, k2tog, k9, sl 1, turn, k to end.

instructions

CENTER LACE SQUARE

With waste yarn make a provisional cast-on of 123 sts. (See Provisional Cast-On, page 121.)

With A, beginning with a RS (knit) row work in St st for 2 rows.

Begin Lace pattern:

Work Diamond Lace Pattern rows 1–16, 12 times.

Work rows 1 and 2 once more.

Knit 1 row decreasing 3 sts spaced evenly across the row—120 sts.

Purl 1 row.

Do not bind off, leaving sts on the needle for the border.

Pick up and knit 150 sts across side edge and with a tapestry needle and waste yarn place sts on waste yarn. (See Picking up Stitches, page 122.)

Pick up and knit 120 sts from the bottom and place on a separate waste yarn.

Pick up and knit 150 sts from the other side and place on waste yarn.

DIAMOND LACE BORDER

With waste yarn make a provisional cast-on of 19 sts.

With B, beginning with row 10 RS of Border Lace Pattern, repeat rows 1–20, ending with row 9. At the end of every even row, knit the last st of border and the next st from Center Lace Square tbl tog. On next row, and every odd row, slip the first st purlwise. When you reach the end of the sts on the needle, follow the instructions for turning the corner (below). Return the next 150 sts to the needle from the waste yarn and repeat the border. Continue in this manner until all four sides are completed.

TURN CORNER

Follow Diamond Lace Border Corner instructions Rows 1–12.

When all four sides are completed, remove the provisional cast-on from border and join the edges with Kitchener St.

FINISHING

Block piece to the finished measurements. Weave in ends.

Rectangle Lace Wrap

materials and tools

Artyarns Silk Essence (100% silk; 1.6oz/45g = 400yd/366m): (A), 1 skein, color #H27—approx 400yd/366m of superfine yarn

Artyarns Beaded Silk & Sequins Light (100% silk w/ Murano glass beads & sequins, 1.76oz/50g = 110 yd/100m): (A), 1 skein, color H27S—approx 110yd/100m of lightweight yarn

Knitting needles: 3.5mm (size 4 U.S.) or size to obtain gauge

Tapestry needle

gauge

20 sts/24 rows = 4"/10cm in Pattern using A, blocked

Always take time to check your gauge.

special abbreviation

Cdd (center double decrease): Slip 2, knit 1, pass slipped stitches over.

finished measurements

12" x 56"/30cm x 142cm, blocked

Here's a romantic and light-weight silk lace wrap that can be worn over the shoulders or around the neck. Containing easy-to-knit lace, the piece has just a few repetitive rows, and the end result looks much more complicated than it really is.

**design by
Iris Schreier**

**skill level
intermediate**

instructions

With B, CO 61 sts.

Knit 1 row with B.

Refer to chart at right for pattern repeat (optional).

Attach A.

Row 1: With A, [k1, yo, k1, ssk, k5, k2tog, k1, yo] 5 times, k1.

Row 2 and all even rows: K1, p to last st, k1. Carry B along side, twisting it around A before starting next row.

Row 3: With A, [k2, yo, k1, ssk, k3, k2tog, k1, yo, k1] 5 times, k1.

Row 5: With A, [k3, yo, k1, ssk, k1, k2tog, k1, yo, k2] 5 times, k1.

Row 7: With A, [k4, yo, k1, cdd, k1, yo, k3] 5 times, k1.

Rows 9-10: With B, k across.

Repeat Rows 1–10, 34 more times, for a total of 35 times.

Then repeat Rows 1–9. Bind off loosely with B.

FINISHING

Weave in ends.

pattern chart

		O		⋀		O						7
	O		/			\		O				5
O		/					\		O			3
O		/					\		O			1

12   10   8   6   4   2

⋀	cdd
\	ssk
/	k2tog
☐	knit on RS
O	yo

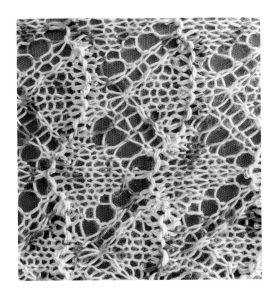

Chella Cowl

Worked in the round from the bottom up, this cowl is larger on the bottom so it sits nicely on the shoulders, then gets smaller to hug up around the neck. It has a simple cable pattern that adds texture and depth without distracting from the pretty beaded yarn.

design by
Jennifer Wood

skill level
intermediate

materials and tools

Artyarns Ultrabulky (100% Italian merino wool; 3.2oz/100g = 110yd/101m): (A), 1 skein, color #247—approx 110yd/100m of bulky yarn **(5)**

Artyarns Beaded Silk & Sequins Light (100% silk w/ Murano glass beads & sequins; 1.76oz/50g = 110yd/100m): (B), 1 skein, color 247G—approx 110yd/100m of lightweight yarn **(3)**

Knitting needles: 7mm or size to obtain gauge

Tapestry needle

gauge

13 sts/18 rows = 4"/10cm in Stockinette Stitch with two strands together, one of each color.

Always take time to check your gauge.

finished measurements

20"/50cm top circumference, 26"/66cm bottom circumference, 6"/15cm tall

pattern chart

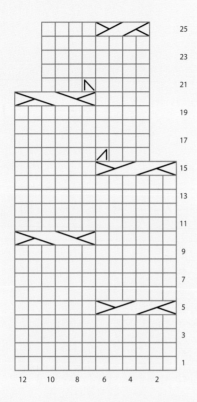

instructions

NOTES: *Use two strands together, one of each yarn, throughout.*

With both yarns held tog, CO 96 sts. Place marker (pm) and join, being careful not to twist the sts.

Purl 3 rnds.

Work Rows 1–25 of Cowl Chart, working 8 repeats in each round.

NOTE: *The stitch count is reduced to 80 sts in Round 16 and to 64 sts in Round 21.*

Purl 3 rnds.

BO purlwise.

FINISHING

Weave in ends.

☐ knit

◪ ssk, return st to left needle, pass the next st over it and off the needle, then slip st back to right needle (2 sts decreased).

◪ sl 1 st purlwise, k2tog, pass slipped st over the k2tog (2 sts decreased).

⬡ sl 2 sts onto cn and hold to back, k2 from left needle, k2 from cn.

⬡ sl 3 sts onto cn and hold to back, k3 from left needle, k3 from cn.

⬡ sl 3 sts onto cn and hold to front, k3 from left needle, k3 from cn.

Textured Reversible Cowl

materials and tools

Artyarns Beaded Silk & Sequins Light (100% silk w/Murano glass beads & sequins; 1.76oz/50g = 110 yd/100m): (A), 1 skein, color 167S—approx 110yd/100m of lightweight yarn

Artyarns Ultrabulky (100% Italian merino wool; 3.2oz/100g = 110yd/101m): (A), 1 skein, color #250—approx 110yd/100m of bulky yarn

Knitting needles: 10mm (size 15 U.S.) and 12.75mm (size 17 U.S.) 16"/40cm circular needle or size to obtain gauge

Cable needle

Tapestry needle

gauge

13 sts/15 rows = 4"/10cm in Moss Stitch Cable pattern

Always take time to check your gauge.

finished measurements

22"/56cm around x 9"/23cm tall

Worked in a two-sided cable pattern, this cowl is fun to knit. A luxurious yarn adds sophistication and style.

design by
Tanya Alpert

skill level
intermediate

pattern stitches

1 X 1 RIB PATTERN
(MULTIPLE OF 2 STS)

Row 1: *K1, p1, rep from * to end of round.

Repeat Round 1 for 1x1 Rib pattern.

MOSS STITCH CABLE PATTERN
(MULTIPLE OF 12 STS)

Rnd 1: *(K1, p1) twice, slip next 4 sts onto cable needle (cn) and hold in front, k1, p1, k1, p1, then k1, p1, k1, p1 from cn, rep from * to end of round.

Rnd 2: *K1, p1, rep from * to end of round.

Rnds 3 and 4: *P1, k1, rep from * to end of round.

Rnd 5: *Sl 4 sts onto cn and hold in back, k1, p1, k1, p1, then k1, p1, k1, p1 from cn, (k1, p1) twice, repeat from * to end of round.

Rnds 6-8: Repeat Rounds 2–4.

Repeat Rounds 1 through 8 for Moss Stitch Cable pattern. Refer to chart, if you prefer.

instructions

With smaller needles and one strand each of A and B held together, CO 72 sts. Place marker (pm), join in the round.

Work in 1x1 Rib pattern for 4 rounds.

Change to larger needle.

Beginning with Round 1, work in Moss Stitch Cable pattern until piece measures 9"/23cm from cast-on edge. End with Round 6.

Bind off loosely.

FINISHING

Weave in all the ends.

Block lightly.

pattern chart

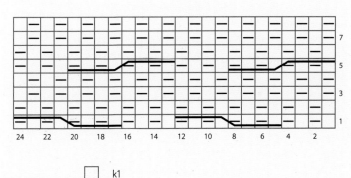

24 22 20 18 16 14 12 10 8 6 4 2

☐ k1

⊟ p1

sl 4 sts to cn, hold in front, (k1, p1) x 2, (k1, p1) x 2 from cn

sl 4 sts to cn, hold back, (k1, p1) x 2, (k1, p1) x 2 from cn

Spiral Cowl

Simple stripes add beauty and intrigue to this basic cowl. Take care weaving in your ends and the piece will be fluid and reversible.

design by
Heather Walpole

skill level
easy

materials and tools

Artyarns Cashmere 3 (100% cashmere; 1.76oz/50g = 170yd/155m): (A), 1 skein, color #134— approx 170yd/155m of light weight yarn

Artyarns Beaded Pearl (100% silk w/Murano glass beads; 1.76oz/50g = 100yd/91m): (B), 1 skein, color #224S—approx 110yd/91m of medium weight yarn

Knitting needles: 4 mm (size 6 U.S.) 24"/60cm circular knitting needle

Stitch marker

Darning needle

Tapestry needle

gauge

22 sts/40 rows = 4"/10cm in Diagonal Rib Stitch

Always take time to check your gauge.

finished measurements

5"/13cm wide x 36"/91 circumference

pattern stitch

**DIAGONAL RIB STITCH
(MULTIPLE OF 8 STS)**

Rnd 1: *K4, p4, rep from * around.

Rnd 2: P1, *k4, p4, rep from * ending p3.

Rnd 3: P2, *k4, p4, rep from * ending p2.

Rnd 4: P3, *k4, p4, rep from * ending p1.

Rnd 5: *P4, k4, rep from * around.

Rnd 6: K1, *p4, k4, rep from * ending k3.

Rnd 7: K2, *p4, k4, rep from * ending k2.

Rnd 8: K3, *p4, k4, rep from * ending k1.

instructions

Using A, CO 192 sts. Place marker and
join in the round, being careful not
to twist cast-on sts.

Work Rnds 1–4 of Diagonal Rib Stitch.

Change to B and work Rnds 5–8 of
Diagonal Rib Stitch.

Repeat these 8 rnds 5 times more.

Change to A and work Rnds 1–4 of
Diagonal Rib Stitch.

Bind off loosely as for Rnd 5.

You may even go up a needle size or
two to achieve a stretchy bind-off.

FINISHING

Weave in ends.

Double Eyelet Lace Cowl

materials and tools

Artyarns Beaded Ensemble (75% silk, 25% cashmere; 3.5oz/100g = 167yd/153m): (A), 1 skein, color #160 Silver—approx 167yd/153m of medium weight yarn

Artyarns Cashmere Sock Yarn (67% cashmere, 25% wool, 8% nylon; 1.76oz/50g = 160yd/146m): (B), 1 skein, color #320—approx 160yd/146m of lightweight yarn

Knitting needles: 4 mm (size 6 U.S.) 16"/40cm circular needle or size to obtain gauge, spare 16" circular needle same size or smaller

Waste yarn

Crochet hook 4mm (G-6)

Stitch marker

Tapestry needle

gauge

19 sts/32 rows = 4"/10cm in pattern stitch with A, before blocking

22 sts/30 rows = 4"/10 cm in Stockinette stitch with A, before blocking

Always take time to check your gauge.

note

If row gauge is off, then more yarn may be used for each round; and the result will be shorter.

finished measurements

22"/56cm circumference x 8¾"/22cm wide

A luscious, warm, and soft knit with a bit of sparkle, this double-sided cowl has the same eyelet lace pattern on both sides.

design by
Nichole Reese

skill level
intermediate

pattern stitch

DOUBLE EYELET LACE PATTERN (MULTIPLE OF 12 STS)

Rnds 1, 2, 3, 5, 6, and 7: *P2, k3, p2, k5, rep from * to end of rnd.

Rnd 4: *P2, k1, yo, ssk, p2, k2tog, yo, k1, yo, ssk, rep from * to end of rnd.

Rnd 8: *P2, k2tog, yo, k1, p2, k2tog, yo, k1, yo, ssk, rep from * to end of rnd.

Rep Rnds 1–8 for Double Eyelet pattern.

instructions

With waste yarn, using crochet hook provisional cast-on, CO 108 sts. (See Provisional Cast-On, page 121.) Join A and k1 rnd. PM and join in the rnd, being careful not to twist.

Work Rnds 1–8 of Double Eyelet Lace pattern 8 times (about 8¾"), then Rnds 1–3 once more.

P1 rnd.

Break yarn, leaving 6"/15cm tail.

Switch to B and k 1 rnd.

Work Rnds 2–8 of Double Eyelet Lace pattern.

Work Rnds 1–8 of Double Eyelet Lace pattern 7 times, then work Rnds 1–3 once more.

P1 rnd.

Break yarn leaving an 80"/203cm tail.

Sew in all ends to WS, except for 80"/203cm tail.

FINISHING

With spare needle, begin removing waste yarn from provisional cast-on, one stitch at a time and placing each st on needle. Once all the sts are on spare needle, push color B section inside color A. Hold the color A and color B sections with WS together and RS of color B facing you, begin Kitchener St with 80"/203cm tail and work all the way around bottom of cowl. Weave in ends.

pattern chart

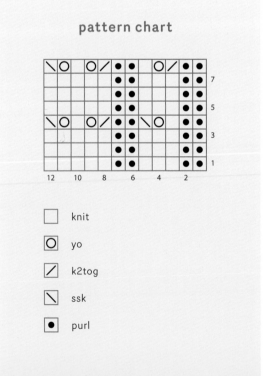

			knit
	O		yo
	/		k2tog
	\		ssk
	•		purl

Reversible Vintage Cowl

materials and tools

Artyarns Cashmere Sock (67% cashmere, 25% wool, 8% nylon; 1.76oz/50g = 160yd/146m): (A), 1 skein, color hot pink #H1; (B), 1 skein, color chocolate brown #248—approx 320yd/293m of lightweight yarn

Knitting needles: 4mm (size 6 U.S.) 16"/40cm circular needles or size to obtain gauge

Stitch marker

Tapestry needle

gauge

17 sts/28 rows = 4"/10cm in double knit pattern

Always take time to check your gauge.

special abbreviations

Kfb: Knit in front and back of same stitch.

Make Bobble (MB): Knit in front of next st without removing from needle, then kfb twice in same st and remove from needle. Turn work to WS, p5, turn, k5, turn, p5, turn, k5. Pass 4th st knit over last st knit, pass over 3rd st, then 2nd st then 1st st over last st; 1 st. Position bobble close to last st, pull yarn tight to secure.

Wyib: With both yarns in back .

Wyif: With both yarns in front.

finished measurements

17"/43cm circumference x 4¼"/11cm high, blocked

This cowl is double knit in the round to create a reversible piece that can be worn inside and out, one side being bright and fun, while the other side is subtle and subdued. Double-layered, it can also be worn as a headband and will keep ears warm even in the coldest of climates. Vibrant colors on cashmere . . . what's not to like?

design by
Lisa Ellis

skill level
intermediate

pattern stitches

DOUBLE KNITTING IN THE ROUND

These are the rules of standard double knitting:

All double knitting is worked in pairs. The first stitch in the pair is always the facing-side stitch, is always knit, and is always worked with all active ends in back (wyib). The second stitch in the pair is always the opposite-side stitch, is always purled, is always worked with the active ends in front (wyif), AND is always worked in the opposite color from the facing-side stitch.

In other words, a pair is worked thus:

Wyib, with A, k1; wyif, with B, pl.

PURL ROUND

Bring B to front of work and place A in back of work. Working opposite color seen, work front sts in purl and work back sts in knit to create purl sts on both sides of work with opposite color as st below.

STRETCHY BIND-OFF

K1, work yo (back to front), *k1, pass yo over k1, pass first knit st over last knit st; rep from* across.

instructions

With B, CO 140 sts. Place marker (pm) and join, being careful not to twist the sts.

Next rnd: *P1, k1; rep from* around.

Attach A and beg double knitting.

Rnds 1–5: Double knit wyib, with A, k1; wyif, with B, pl.

Rnd 6: Work double knit pattern to 3rd st , using A, MB in 3rd st, continue double knitting to 41st st, using A, MB in 41st st, continue double knitting to 85th st, using A, MB in 85th st, continue double knitting to end of rnd—3 bobbles made on A side only.

Rnd 7: Work purl rnd.

Rnds 8–12: Double knit wyib, with A, k1; wyif, with B, pl.

Rnd 13: Work purl rnd.

Rnd 14: Double knit wyib, with A, k1; wyif, with B, pl.

Rnd 15: Work double knit pattern to 21st st, using A, MB in 21st st, continue double knitting to 63rd st, using A, MB in 63rd st, continue double knitting to 113th st, using A, MB in 113th st, continue double knitting to end of rnd—3 bobbles made on A side only.

Rnds 16–18: Double knit wyib, with A, k1; wyif, with B, pl.

Rnd 19: Work purl rnd.

Rnd 20: Double knit wyib, with A, k1; wyif, with B, pl.

Rnd 21: Work double knit pattern to 53rd st, using A, MB in 53rd st, continue double knitting to 87th st, using A, MB in 87th st, continue double knitting to 128th st, using A, MB in 128th st, continue double knitting to end of rnd—3 bobbles made on A side only.

Rnds 22–25: Double knit wyib, with A, k1; wyif, with B, pl. Cut A.

Rnd 26: With B, *k2tog; rep from* around—70 sts.

Rnd 27: With B, knit around.

BO all sts using the Stretchy Bind-Off.

Cut yarn, draw tail through rem st and secure.

FINISHING

Weave in ends through center of cowl. Block lightly.

Fallen Halo

A welting pattern is created in the Fallen Halo by a number of knit rows followed by a number of purl rows. Alternating purl rows of a yarn with a bit of glitter with knit rows of a soft, cashmere yarn creates a luxurious combination of thickness and texture with a little added sparkle.

design by
Pam Grushkin

skill level
beginner
● ● ● ●

materials and tools

Artyarns Cashmere Glitter (100% cashmere plied with metallic thread; 1.76oz/50g = 170yd/155m): (A), 1 skein, color # H-14G—approx 170yd/155m of lightweight yarn (3)

Artyarns Cashmere 5 (100% cashmere; 1.76oz/50g = 102yd/93m): (B), 1 skein, color # H-14—approx 102yd/93m of medium weight yarn (4)

Knitting needles: 4.5mm (size 7 U.S.) 24"/60cm circular or size to obtain gauge

Stitch marker

Tapestry needle

gauge

16 sts/56 rounds (unstretched) = 4"/10cm using A in circular welt pattern

Always take time to check your gauge.

finished measurements

20"/51cm at cast-on, 9"/23cm deep, 25"/63.5cm at bind-off. One size fits all.

instructions

CO 81 sts, loosely with A. Being careful not to twist sts, join in the rnd as follows: sl last st cast on from rhn to lhn, place marker (pm) on rhn, p2tog to join.

Purl 9 rnds.

*Change to B. Always twist yarns at beg of rnd (here and throughout pattern) and pull tight after knitting first st of rnd, to avoid holes.

K 6 rnds.

Next rnd: Inc 3 sts evenly across rnd—84 sts.

Change to A. P 9 rnds*.

Rep from * to * 6 times for a total of 7 times—102 sts. BO loosely using B.

FINISHING

Weave ends. Gently steam block to measurements, if necessary.

Stranded Loop Cowl

This cowl uses a pattern that doesn't require catching floats behind the work, so it's a great first stranded colorwork project.

design by
Samantha Glenn

skill level
easy

materials and tools

TSCArtyarns Cashmere Tweed (85% merino wool, 15% cashmere; 3.2oz/90g = 340yd/311m): (A), 1 skein, color # CT-12, held double throughout—approx 340yd/311m of lightweight yarn (3)

TSCArtyarns Vanessa (60% merino wool, 40% super kid mohair, 3.5oz/100g = 196yd/179m): (B), 1 skein, color # V-19—approx 196yd/179m of medium weight yarn (4)

Knitting needles: 5mm (size 9 U.S.) 16"/40cm circular needles or size to obtain gauge

Crochet hook for provisional cast-on

4 stitch markers

Waste yarn

Tapestry needle

gauge

21½ sts/18 rows = 4"/10cm in color chart after blocking

Always take time to check your gauge.

finished measurements

26"/66cm circumference x 6¾"/17cm wide

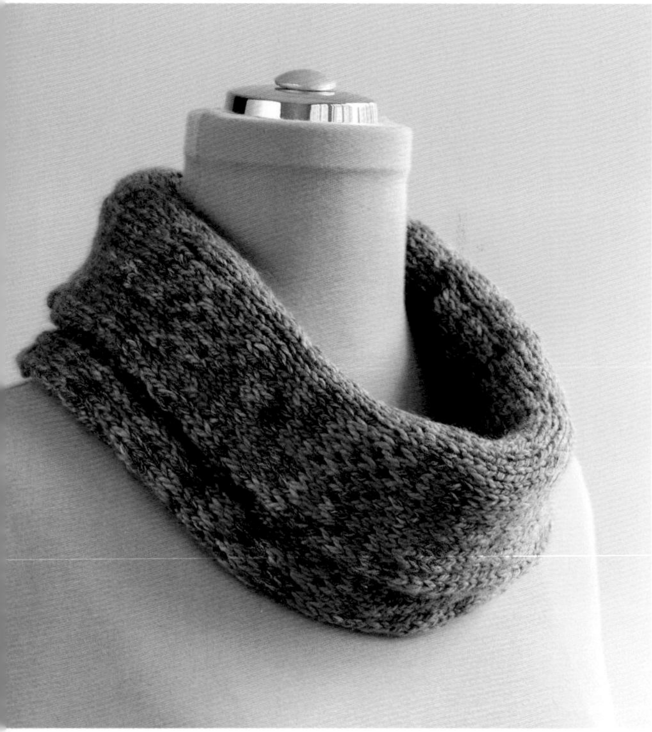

pattern chart

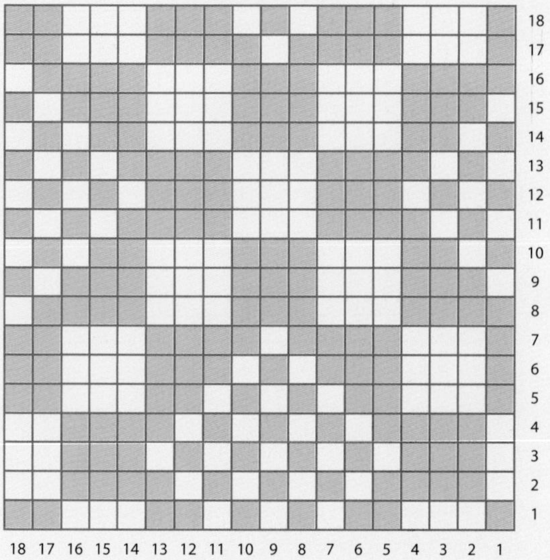
18
17
16
15
14
13
12
11
10
9
8
7
6
5
4
3
2
1
18 17 16 15 14 13 12 11 10 9 8 7 6 5 4 3 2 1

instructions

Using a provisional cast-on, CO 72 sts. (See Provisional Cast-On, page 121.) Starting with round 1, and using colors A and B, follow chart to end, repeating chart 4 times around. Place a marker after each repeat to easily keep track of where you are. PM, join in the round, and continue with chart to round 18, slipping all markers.

Complete a total of 7 chart repeats.

FINISHING

Place live stitches on waste yarn, tying ends of waste yarn together securely. Wet block piece to measurements. When completely dry, place live stitches onto two needles, remove waste yarn, and graft the two ends together using Kitchener St as follows: With wrong sides of the knitted fabric that you're joining facing each other, hold the 2 needles together in your left hand. Using the tail from one of the needles, thread it through a tapestry needle. Insert tapestry needle purlwise through first st on needle closest to you. Pull through, but don't take the st off the needle.

Then thread the tapestry needle knitwise through the first st on the needle farthest from you. Pull through, but keep the st on the needle. *(1) Thread the tapestry needle knitwise through the 1st st on the needle closest to you. Take the st off the needle. Pull through. (2) Thread the tapestry needle purlwise through the first st on the needle farthest from you. Take the st off the needle. Thread the tapestry needle knitwise through the next st on that same needle. Pull through. Rep from * until there are no more sts rem. Weave in ends.

Quilted Cowl

materials and tools

Artyarns Rhapsody Light (85% silk, 15% mohair; 2.82oz/80g = 400yd/366m): (A), 1 skein, color# 205—approx 400yd/366m of lightweight yarn 3

Artyarns Beaded Ensemble and Sequins (75% silk, 25% cashmere w/ Lurex & silk-strung Murano glass beads & sequins; 3.5oz/100g = 128yd/117m): (B), 1 skein, color # 205—approx 128yd/117m of medium weight yarn 4

Knitting needles: 4mm (size 6 U.S.) needles or size to obtain gauge

Tapestry needle

gauge

24 sts/40 rows = 4"/10cm using A and B in Quilted Pattern

Always take time to check your gauge.

finished measurements

8½"/22cm high x 15"/38cm wide

The Quilted Cowl is a twisted piece that shows both sides of the quilted pattern. It is worked in the round and is completely seamless.

design by
Laura Zukaite

skill level
intermediate

pattern stitch

QUILTED PATTERN (MULTIPLE OF 6 STS)

Rnds 1, 2, and 3: Using B, *k4, sl 2 wyib; repeat from *.

Rnd 4: Using A, knit.

Rnd 5: Using A, purl.

Rnds 6, 7, and 8: Using B, k1, * sl 2 wyib, k4; repeat from *, end k3.

Rnd 9: Using A, knit.

Rnd 10: Using A, purl.

Rep Rnds 1–10 for Quilted Pattern.

instructions

Using 2 strands of A, CO 180 sts, PM and join in the round twisting the first row.

Setup Row 1: Purl.

Setup Row 2: Knit.

Setup Row 3: Purl.

Work in Quilted Pattern until piece measures 8½"/22cm ending with pattern Row 10.

BO all sts loosely in A.

FINISHING

Block to final measurements. Weave in the ends.

Sheer Rounds Shoulder Capelet

materials and tools

TSCArtyarns Zara Hand-Dyed (100% extrafine merino wool; 3.5oz/100g = 240yd/219m): (A), 1 skein, color # Z-16—approx 240yd/219m of lightweight yarn (3)

TSCArtyarns Tranquility (60% extrafine merino wool, 25% cashmere, 15% silk; 2oz/57g = 400yd/366m): (B), 1 skein, color # T/6—approx 400yd/366m of lightweight yarn (3)

Knitting needles: 5.5mm (size 9 U.S.) 24"/60cm circular needle or size to obtain gauge

1 stitch marker

Tapestry needle

Optional: row counter

gauge

18 sts/22 rows = 4"/10cm in Stockinette Stitch worked in rnds with both yarns held tog

Always take time to check your gauge.

special abbreviation

Kfb: Knit in front and back of same stitch.

notes

1. You will be working with the two yarns held together, unless noted.

2. Sheer rounds are worked with B only. When working with B only, do not cut A; carry A up, catching it in the first st of each round of Garter St.

finished measurements

13"/33cm wide (at center) x 17"/43cm long, after light steaming; measurements are approximate

This capelet graces the neck and upper body, sloping slightly off the shoulders, which gives it a very feminine and stylish appearance. The lighter-weight yarn is used on its own to create bands of sheer rounds that grow longer as the cowl extends over the shoulders.

design by
Laurie Kimmelstiel

skill level
easy

instructions

With both yarns held tog, CO 91 sts, move the first stitch on right needle to left needle, place marker on right needle and k2tog, continue to knit in the round for 1 round—90 sts.

Rnd 2: Purl.

Rnds 3–11: Knit 9 rnds.

Rnd 12: *K17, kfb, rep from* around—95 sts.

Drop A, but do not cut.

FIRST SHEER ROUNDS

Working with B only and beginning with a purl round, work in Garter St (purl 1 rnd, knit 1 rnd) for 4 rounds.

Resume working with both A and B held tog.

Rnd 1: Purl.

Rnds 2–4: Knit.

Rnd 5: *K18, kfb, rep from* around—100 sts.

Rnds 6–10: Knit.

Rnd 11: *K19, kfb, rep from* around—105 sts.

Drop A, but do not cut.

SECOND SHEER ROUNDS

Working with B only and beginning with a purl round, work in Garter St for 6 rounds.

Resume working with both A and B held tog.

Rnd 1: Purl.

Rnds 2–4: Knit.

Rnd 5: *K20, kfb, rep from* around—110 sts.

Rnds 6–10: Knit.

THIRD SHEER ROUNDS

Working with B only and beginning with a purl round, work in Garter St for 8 rounds.

Resume working with both A and B held tog.

Rnd 1: Purl.

Rnds 2–4: Knit.

Rnd 5: *K10, kfb, rep from* across round—120 sts.

Rnds 6–10: Knit.

FOURTH SHEER ROUNDS

Working with B only and beginning with a purl round, work in Garter St for 10 rounds.

Resume working with both A and B held tog.

Rnd 1: Purl.

Rnds 2–4: Knit.

Rnd 5: *K11, kfb, rep from* around—130 sts.

Rnds 6–10: Knit.

Rnd 11: Purl.

Rnd 12: Knit.

Bind off carefully and loosely purlwise. If your bind off appears too tight, consider using a larger needle.

FINISHING

Lightly steam press or block as desired. This pattern will naturally "crunch up" onto itself without blocking , but it looks great with or without blocking. Weave in ends.

Earth and Sky Capelet

A sequence of lace motifs circling its border turn this simple cashmere capelet into a luxurious fashion accessory. I call this the Earth and Sky Capelet because the Twin Leaf Lace and Vine Lace patterns along the bottom edge remind me of tree trunks and wild vines reaching upward toward the sky.

design by
Laurie Kimmelstiel

skill level
intermediate

materials and tools

Artyarns Cashmere 2 (100% cashmere; 1.76oz/50g = 255yd/233m): (A), 1 skein, color # H33; (B), 1 skein, color #261—approx 255yd/233m fine weight yarn (**2**)

Knitting needles: 3.25 mm (Size 3 U.S.) 24"/60cm circular needle or size to obtain gauge

11 stitch markers

Optional: row counter

Tapestry needle

gauge

24 sts/28 rows = approx 4"/10cm in Stockinette Stitch worked in rnds

Always take time to check your gauge.

special abbreviations

Kfb: Knit in front and back of same stitch.

Pfb: Purl in front and back of same stitch.

finished measurements

15"/38cm long and 19"/48cm neck circumference, unstretched; measurements taken after blocking and are approximate

note

This capelet incorporates the Vine Lace Pattern and an interpretation of the Twin Leaf Lace Pattern from *A Treasury of Knitting Patterns* by Barbara G. Walker (Schoolhouse Press, 1998). Used with permission by Schoolhouse Press.

pattern stitches

**VINE LACE PATTERN
(MULTIPLE OF 9 STS + 4)**

Rnd 1: Knit.

Rnd 2: K3, *yo, k2, ssk, k2tog, k2, yo, k1; rep from * to last st, k1.

Rnd 3: Knit.

Rnd 4: K2, *yo, k2, ssk, k2tog, k2, yo, k1; rep from * to last 2 sts, k2.

**TWIN LEAF LACE PATTERN
(MULTIPLE OF 23 STS)**

Rnd 1: *K8, k2tog, yo, k1, p1, k1, yo, ssk, k8, rep from * around.

Rnd 2: *K7, k2tog tbl, k2, yo, p1, yo, k2, k2tog, k7, rep from * around.

Rnd 3: *K6, k2tog, k1, yo, k2, p1, k2, yo, k1, ssk, k6, rep from * around.

Rnd 4: *K5, k2tog tbl, k3, yo, k1, p1, k1, yo, k3, ssk, k5, rep from * around.

Rnd 5: *K4, k2tog, k2, yo, k3, p1, k3, yo, k2, ssk, k4, rep from * around.

Rnd 6: *K3, k2tog tbl, k4, yo, k2, p1, k2, yo, k4, k2tog, k3, rep from * around.

Rnd 7: *K2, k2tog, k3, yo, k4, p1, k4, yo, k3, ssk, k2, rep from * around.

Rnd 8: *K1, k2tog tbl, k5, yo, k3, p1, k3, yo, k5, k2tog, k1, rep from * around.

Rnd 9: *K2tog, k4, yo, k5, p1, k5, yo, k4, ssk, rep from * around.

Rnds 10–12: *K11, p1, k11, rep from * around.

instructions

With A, CO 114 sts, place marker (pm) and join to knit in the round.

Knit in the round until piece measures ¾"/2cm.

Next rnd (1st increase rnd): *K19, M1, rep from * around—120 sts.

Continue to knit in the round until piece measures 2"/5cm.

Next rnd (2nd increase rnd): *K12, M1, rep from * around—130 sts.

Continue to knit in the round until piece measures approx 3¾"/10cm.

Next rnd (3rd increase rnd): *K13, M1, rep from * around—140 sts.

Continue to knit in the round until piece measures 5¾"/15cm.

Next rnd (4th increase rnd): *K14, M1, rep from * around—150 sts.

Continue to knit in the round until piece measures 7"/18cm.

Next rnd (5th increase rnd): *K15, M1, rep from * around—160 sts.

Continue to knit in the round until piece measures 8"/20cm.

Next rnd (6th increase rnd): *K16, M1, rep from * around—170 sts.

Continue to knit in the round until piece measures 9½"/24cm.

Next rnd (7th increase rnd): *K17, M1, rep from * around—180 sts.

Next rnd: Knit, inc 4 sts evenly around—184 sts.

VINE LACE SECTION

Work Rnds 2-4 of Vine Lace pattern, then Rows 1-4 of pattern once.

Knit 1 rnd.

Next rnd: *K18, M1 rep from * to last 4 sts, k4—194 sts.

Switch to B and knit for 3 rnds.

Next rnd: *K19, M1, rep from * to last 4 sts, k4—204 sts.

Knit 3 rnds.

Next rnd: *K10 M1, rep from * to last 4 sts, k4—224 sts.

Knit 3 rnds.

Next rnd: K1, M1, k7, M1, *k8, M1, rep from * around—253 sts.

TWIN LEAF LACE SECTION

Next rnd: Work Rnd 1 of Twin Leaf Lace pattern, placing markers to delineate each of the 23-st panels.

Continue in Twin Leaf Lace pattern, slipping markers as you come to them, until all 12 rnds have been worked.

BOTTOM BORDER

Rnd 1: *M1P, continue in pattern (knit the knits and purl the purls) to last st before each marker, kfb (the kfb will create a purl st in the st preceding the marker), sm, rep from * around—275 sts.

Rnd 2: *Pfb, continue in pattern to the purl st before marker, pfb, sm, rep from * around—297 sts.

Rnd 3: *P1, pfb, continue in pattern to 2 sts before marker, p1, pfb, sm, rep from * around—319 sts.

Rnd 4: *[Pfb] twice, p1, continue in pattern to 3 sts before marker, [pfb] twice, p1, sm, rep from * around—363 sts.

Rnds 5-7: Knit the knits and purl the purls around. You will have 5 purl sts on each side of each marker. This will create a mini ruffle between the motifs.

Bind off in pattern.

FINISHING

Steam press lightly or you may block and pin to form "points" at the center of the purl stitch ruffles between each Twin Leaf Lace motif panel. Weave in ends.

Manteau Capelet

materials and tools

Artyarns Ensemble Light (50% cashmere/50% silk; 2.82oz/80g = 400yd/366m): (A): 1 skein, color #H5—approx 400yd/366m of lightweight yarn

Artyarns Beaded Silk & Sequins Light (100% silk w/glass beads & sequins; 1.76oz/50g = 110yd/101m): (B), 1 skein, color #H24g—approx. 110yd/101m of lightweight yarn

Knitting needles: 6mm (size 10 U.S.) 16"/40cm circular needle, 24"/60cm circular needle or size to obtain gauge

Stitch marker

Tapestry needle

gauge

14½ sts/26 rnds = 4"/10cm in Stockinette st worked in rnds using A

Always take time to check your gauge.

Work a mock in-the-round swatch as follows: With circular needle, CO 20 sts. Work a complete right side row. Next, slide the sts to the opposite end of the circular (like when working an I-cord) and place that needle in your LH. Carry the yarn very loosely behind the swatch (the strand of yarn has to be very loose to avoid distorting the swatch) and work another row. Rep until your swatch is at least 4"/10cm tall. Center 2"/5cm = 7.25sts; the edge sts will be really loose and are not included in measuring the gauge.

special abbreviation

Kfb: Knit in front and back of same stitch.

note

This capelet is knit from the top down.

finished measurements

23"/58cm at neck edge, 15"/38cm deep, and 45"/114cm at bottom, unblocked

The sparkle of the yarn in this simple and elegant capelet frames your neck like a beautiful necklace and adds the perfect finishing touch to the bottom border. The pattern repeat is easy to remember and combines a subtle feather and fan stitch with a defining eyelet row.

design by
Pam Grushkin

skill level
intermediate

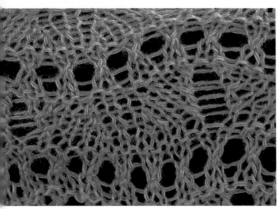

instructions

With 16"/40cm circular, CO 83 sts loosely, with A. Being careful not to twist sts, join in the rnd as follows: Sl last st cast on from RH needle to LH needle, place marker (pm) on RH needle, p2tog to join—82 sts. Cut A.

Join B and work as follows:

Rnd 1: Purl.

Rnds 2 and 3: Knit.

Rnd 4: *Yo, k2tog, rep from * around.

Rnd 5: *K1, k1tbl, rep from * around.

Rnd 6: K6, M1, (k14, M1) 5 times, k6—88 sts.

Rnd 7: Purl.

Rnd 8: Knit.

Rnd 9: *K2tog, k2, kfb, k1, kfb, k2, k2tog tbl; rep from * around.

Rnds 10 and 12: Knit.

Rnds 11 and 13: Rep rnd 9.

Rnd 14: K7, M1, (k15, M1) 5 times, k6—94 sts.

Cut B. Rejoin A. Switch to 24"/60cm circular when sts become too crowded.

Rnds 15-19: Rep Rnds 1-5.

Rnd 20: K9, M1, (k19, M1) 4 times, k9—99 sts.

Rnds 21-27: Rep Rnds 7-13.

Rnd 28: K12, M1, (k19, M1) 4 times, k11—104 sts.

Rnds 29-33: Rep rnds 1-5.

Rnd 34: K10, M1, (k17, M1) 5 times, k9—110 sts.

Rnds 35-41: Rep Rnds 7-13.

Rnd 42: K10, M1, (k18, M1) 5 times, k10—116 sts.

Rnds 43-47: Rep Rnds 1-5.

Rnd 48: K12, M1, (k23, M1) 4 times, k12—121 sts.

Rnds 49-55: Rep Rnds 7-13.

Rnd 56: K13, M1, (k24, M1) 4 times, k12—126 sts.

Rnds 57-61: Rep Rnds 1-5.

Rnd 62: K11, M1, (k21, M1) 5 times, k10—132 sts.

Rnds 63-69: Rep Rnds 7-13.

Rnd 70: K11, M1, (k22, M1) 5 times, k11—138 sts.

Rnds 71-75: Rep Rnds 1-5.

Rnd 76: K13, M1, (k28, M1) 4 times, k13—143 sts.

Rnds 77-83: Rep Rnds 7-13.

Rnd 84: K1, M1, knit even to end of rnd—144 sts.

Rnds 85-89: Rep Rnds 1-5.

Rnd 90: Knit.

Rnd 91: Purl.

Rnd 92: Knit.

Cut A. Rejoin B.

Rnd 1: Purl.

Rnd 2: Knit.

Rep rnds 1 and 2 three times more.

BO purlwise, using Jeny's Surprisingly Elastic BO (see page 123). Cut yarn and pull through last st.

FINISHING

Weave ends. Gently steam block to measurements, if necessary.

Beaded Eyelet Hug

materials and tools

Artyarns Rhapsody Light (85% silk, 15% kid mohair; 2.82oz/80g = 400yd/366m): (A), 1 skein, color # H2—approx 400yd/366m of lightweight yarn

Artyarns Beaded Pearl & Sequins (100% silk w/beads & sequins, 1.76oz/50g = 80yd/73m): (B), 1 skein, color # H2G—approx 80yd/73m of medium weight yarn

Knitting needles: 4mm (size 6 U.S.) 24"/60cm circular needle or size to obtain gauge

6 stitch markers, one a unique color

Tapestry needle

gauge

20 sts/24 rows = 4"/10cm in Stockinette Stitch using A

Always take time to check your gauge.

finished measurements

21½"/55cm around at top, 12½"/32cm long and about 50"/127cm around at bottom edge

This versatile hug is knit in the round from the top down with a luscious yarn and is highlighted by beads and sequins. The increased shaping is hidden in the eyelet design.

design by
Nell Ziroli

skill level
easy

instructions

Join tails of both yarns together with a slip knot; do not count the slip knot as a stitch.

CO 108 sts using long tail method, holding A over thumb and B over finger. This will make the loops in B and the bottom wrap in A.

Do not cut A. Remove slip knot. Join in the round, taking care not to twist; place unique marker for beginning of round.

With B, knit 2 rnds, purl 1 rnd, and knit 1 rnd.

With A, knit 1 rnd.

BAND PATTERN

With A, work the following 6 rnds for Band Pattern.

Rnds 1 and 5: *K2, skp, yo, k1, yo, k2tog, k2; rep from * around.

Rnds 2 and 4: Knit.

Rnd 3: *K2, yo, skp, k1, k2tog, yo, k2; rep from * around.

Rnd 6: Knit.

With B, knit 1 rnd and purl 1 rnd. Cut B.

Next rnd: With A, [k18, place marker] 5 times, k18—markers placed to divide work into 6 sections.

Slip markers as you come to them.

BEGIN MAIN SECTION PATTERN

Rnd 1: *K3, yo, k1, yo, k14, rep from * around—120 sts.

Rnds 2 and 3: Knit.

Rnd 4: *K2, yo, skp, k1, k2tog, yo, k to marker, rep from * around.

Rnd 5: *K4, yo, k1, yo, k to marker, rep from * around—132 sts.

Rnds 6 and 7: Knit.

Rnd 8: *K5, yo, k1, yo, k to marker, rep from * around—144 sts.

Rnds 9 and 11: Knit.

Rnd 10: *K4, yo, skp, k1, k2tog, yo, k to marker, rep from * around.

Rnd 12: *K6, yo, k1, yo, k to marker, rep from * around—156 sts.

Rnds 13–15: Knit.

Rnd 16: *K7, yo, k1, yo, k to marker, rep from * around—168 sts.

Rnds 17 and 19: Knit.

Rnd 18: *K6, yo, skp, k1, k2tog, yo, k to marker, rep from * around.

Rnd 20: *K8, yo, k1, yo, k to marker, rep from * around—180 sts.

Rnds 21, 22, 23, and 24: Knit.

Rnd 25: *K9, yo, k1, yo, k to marker, rep from * around—192 sts.

Rnds 26 and 28: Knit.

Rnd 27: *K8, yo, skp, k1, k2tog, yo, k to marker, rep from * around.

Rnd 29: *K10, yo, k1, yo, k to marker, rep from * around—204 sts.

Rnds 30, 31, 32, 33 and 34: Knit.

Rnd 35: *K11, yo, k1, yo, k to marker, rep from * around—216 sts.

Rnds 36 and 38: Knit.

Rnd 37: *K10, yo, skp, k1, k2tog, yo, k to marker, rep from * around.

Rnd 39: *K12, yo, k1, yo, k to marker, rep from * around—228 sts.

Rnds 40, 41, 42, 43, 44 and 45: Knit.

Rnd 46: *K13, yo, k1, yo, k16, skp, yo, k1, yo, k2tog, k3, rep from * around—240 sts.

Rnds 47 and 49: Knit.

Rnd 48: *K12, yo, skp, k1, k2tog, yo, k15, yo, skp, k1, k2tog, yo, k3, rep from * around.

Rnd 50: *K12, skp, yo, k1, yo, k2tog, k15, skp, yo, k1, yo, k2tog, k3, rep from * around.

Rnds 51-57: Knit.

Rejoin B. Do not cut A.

Rnd 58: With B, knit.

Rnd 59: With B, purl.

Rnd 60: With A, knit.

Rnds 61 and 65: *K2, skp, yo, k1, yo, k2tog, k3, rep from * around.

Rnds 62, 64, 66, and 67: Knit.

Rnd 63: *K2, yo, skp, k1, k2tog, yo, k3, rep from * around.

Rnds 68, 70, and 72: With B, knit.

Rnd 69 and 71: With B, purl.

Cut B.

With A, bind off purlwise.

FINISHING

Weave in ends.

The Versatile Neck Hug offers many possibilities for wear. Not only a neck warmer, it also can cover your shoulders as a hug, or slip over your head as a hood. Wear it as a scarf, add a shawl pin, and you will have a true showstopper! This is an easy-to-work project that involves many delightful hours of knitting and purling.

design by
Judith Rudnick Kane

skill level
easy

Versatile Neck Hug

materials and tools

Artyarns Silk Mohair (60% super kid mohair; 40% silk; 0.88oz/25g = 312yd/285m): (A), 1 skein, color # 251; (B), l skein, color multi #1022— approx 624yd/570m of lace weight yarn

Knitting needles: 3.25 mm (size 3 U.S.) 16"/40cm circular needle, 3.5 mm (size 4 U.S.) 16"/40cm circular needle, 3.75 mm (size 5 U.S.) 16"/4cm circular needle or size to obtain gauge

Tapestry needle

gauge

18 sts/32 rows = 4"/10cm in Stockinette Stitch using 3.75mm (size 5 U.S.) needle

Always take time to check your gauge.

note

You will notice that this pattern uses three different needle sizes to give the garment more versatility. It is lacier on the bottom so that you can wear it as a hug around your shoulders. The top is narrower so that you can create a hood.

finished measurements

29"/74cm circumference at widest, 21"/53cm at narrow end, and 30"/76cm long

pattern stitch

2X2 RIB STRIPES (MULTIPLE OF 4 STS)

Rnd 1: With A, *k2, p2, rep from * around.

Rnd 2: With A, sl 1, k1, p2, *k2, p2, rep from * around.

Rnds 3 and 4: With B, rep rnds 1 and 2.

Rep Rnds 1–4 for 2x2 Rib Stripes pattern.

instructions

With 3.75mm (size 5 U.S.) needle and A, CO 132 sts loosely. Place marker and join, being careful not to twist.

Using 3.75mm (size 5 U.S.) needle, work in 2x2 Rib Stripes pattern for 6"/15cm.

Using 3.5mm (size 4 U.S.) needle, work in 2x2 Rib Stripes pattern for 6"/15cm.

Using 3.25mm (size 3 U.S.) needle, work in 2x2 Rib Stripes pattern until piece measures 30"/76cm from beg or desired length.

BO loosely.

FINISHING

Weave in ends.

Feather Poncho

materials and tools

Artyarns Ensemble 4 (50% silk, 50% cashmere; 2.82oz/80g =200yd/183m): (A), 1 skein, color #H31—approx 200yd/183m of medium weight yarn

Artyarns Ensemble Glitter Light (50% silk, 50% cashmere; 2.82oz/80g= 400yd/366m): (B), 1 skein, color # 904S—approx 400yd/366m of lightweight yarn

Knitting needles: 5.5mm (size 9 U.S.) 16"/40cm circular needle, 5.5mm (size 9 U.S.) 24"/60cm circular needle, 5.5mm (size 9 U.S.) 32"/80cm circular needle, 4.5mm (size 7 U.S.), double pointed needles for finishing neckline or size to obtain gauge.

Tapestry needle

gauge

14 sts/20 rows = 4"/10cm in Stockinette Stitch after blocking.

Always take time to check your gauge.

special abbreviation

Cdd (center double decrease): Slip 2, knit 1, pass slipped stitches over.

notes

1. Make sure to carry yarn not being worked up by twisting over working yarn on each round along wrong side of garment.

2. Change to longer circular needle(s) as number of stitches increase.

finished measurements

100"/254cm circumference, 20"/51cm neck opening, 18"/46cm deep at center

Here's a feathery-light poncho to slip on for a little extra luxurious warmth. This is such a fun top-down piece to knit, because the four quadrants are identical, and the entire piece is knitted in the round. It is easy to get into the rhythm of this knitting, and the resulting garment looks much more complicated than it actually is.

design by
Iris Schreier

skill level
intermediate

pattern stitch

LACE PATTERN (LP) (OVER 10 STS)

Row 1: Yo, ssk, k5, k2tog, yo, k1.

Row 2: K1, yo, ssk, k3, k2tog, yo, k2.

Row 3: K2, yo, ssk, k1, k2tog, yo, k3.

Row 4: K3, yo, cdd, yo, k4.

instructions

With A, CO 68 sts. Join to knit in the round.

From now on instructions are given in quadrants, and each round repeats 4 times around to complete a round.

ATTACH B, AND WORK RNDS 1-4 WITH B.

Rnd 1: K1, yo, k3, LP Row 1, k2, yo, k1.

Rnd 2: K1, yo, k4, LP Row 2, k3, yo, k1.

Rnd 3: K1, yo, k5, LP Row 3, k4, yo, k1.

Rnd 4: K1, yo, k6, LP Row 4, k5, yo, k1.

Rnd 5: With A, k25.

WORK RNDS 6-9 WITH B.

Rnd 6: K1, yo, k7, LP Row 1, k6, yo, k1.

Rnd 7: K1, yo, k8, LP Row 2, k7, yo, k1.

Rnd 8: K1, yo, k9, LP Row 3, k8, yo, k1.

Rnd 9: K1, yo, k10, LP Row 4, k9, yo, k1.

Rnd 10: With A and B held together, k33.

WORK RNDS 11-14 WITH B.

Rnd 11: K1, yo, k1, (LP Row 1) 3 times, yo, k1.

Rnd 12: K1, yo, k2, (LP Row 2) 3 times, k1, yo, k1.

Rnd 13: K1, yo, k3, (LP Row 3) 3 times, k2, yo, k1.

Rnd 14: K1, yo, k4, (LP Row 4) 3 times, k3, yo, k1.

Rnd 15: With A and B together, k41.

WORK RNDS 16-19 WITH B.

Rnd 16: K1, yo, k5, (LP Row 1) 3 times, k4, yo, k1.

Rnd 17: K1, yo, k6, (LP Row 2) 3 times, k5, yo, k1.

Rnd 18: K1, yo, k7, (LP Row 3) 3 times, k6, yo, k1.

Rnd 19: K1, yo, k8, (LP Row 4) 3 times, k7, yo, k1.

Rnd 20: With A and B together, k49.

WORK RNDS 21-24 WITH B.

Rnd 21: K1, yo, k9, (LP Row 1) 3 times, k8, yo, k1.

Rnd 22: K1, yo, k10, (LP Row 2) 3 times, k9, yo, k1.

Rnd 23: K1, yo, k11, (LP Row 3) 3 times, k10, yo, k1.

Rnd 24: K1, yo, k12, (LP Row 4) 3 times, k11, yo, k1.

Rnd 25: With A and B together, k57.

WORK RNDS 26-29 WITH B.

Rnd 26: K1, yo, k3, (LP Row 1) 5 times, k2, yo, k1.

Rnd 27: K1, yo, k4, (LP Row 2) 5 times, k3, yo, k1.

Rnd 28: K1, yo, k5, (LP Row 3) 5 times, k4, yo, k1.

Rnd 29: K1, yo, k6, (LP Row 4) 5 times, k5, yo, k1.

Rnd 30: With A and B together, k65.

WORK RNDS 31-34 WITH B.

Rnd 31: K1, yo, k7, (LP Row 1) 5 times, k6, yo, k1.

Rnd 32: K1, yo, k8, (LP Row 2) 5 times, k7, yo, k1.

Rnd 33: K1, yo, k9, (LP Row 3) 5 times, k8, yo, k1.

Rnd 34: K1, yo, k10, (LP Row 4) 5 times, k9, yo, k1.

Rnd 35: With A and B together, k73.

WORK RNDS 36-39 WITH B.

Rnd 36: K1, yo, k11, (LP Row 1) 5 times, k10, yo, k1.

Rnd 37: K1, yo, k12, (LP Row 2) 5 times, k11, yo, k1.

Rnd 38: K1, yo, k13, (LP Row 3) 5 times, k12, yo, k1.

Rnd 39: K1, yo, k14, (LP Row 4) 5 times, k13, yo, k1.

Rnd 40: With A and B together, k81.

WORK RNDS 41–44 WITH B.

Rnd 41: K1, yo, k5, (LP Row 1) 7 times, k4, yo, k1.

Rnd 42: K1, yo, k6, (LP Row 2) 7 times, k5, yo, k1.

Rnd 43: K1, yo, k7, (LP Row 3) 7 times, k6, yo, k1.

Rnd 44: K1, yo, k8, (LP Row 4) 7 times, k7, yo, k1.

Rnd 45: With A and B together, k89.

WORK RNDS 46–49 WITH B.

Rnd 46: K1, yo, k9, (LP Row 1) 7 times, k8, yo, k1.

Rnd 47: K1, yo, k10, (LP Row 2) 7 times, k9, yo, k1.

Rnd 48: K1, yo, k11, (LP Row 3) 7 times, k10, yo, k1.

Rnd 49: K1, yo, k12, (LP Row 4) 7 times, k11, yo, k1.

Rnd 50: With A and B together, k97.

WORK RNDS 51–54 WITH B.

Rnd 51: K1, yo, k13, (LP Row 1) 7 times, k12, yo, k1.

Rnd 52: K1, yo, k14, (LP Row 2) 7 times, k13, yo, k1.

Rnd 53: K1, yo, k15, (LP Row 3) 7 times, k14, yo, k1.

Rnd 54: K1, yo, k16, (LP Row 4) 7 times, k15, yo, k1.

105 sts total in each quadrant.

FINISHING

BOTTOM EDGING

Cut B. With A alone, bind off as follows: [yo, cdd, yo, k1], turn; k5, turn; BO 5 sts.

Repeat across until all sts have been bound off. Cut yarn.

COLLAR

With right side facing, using double pointed needles and A and B together, working in the round, pick up and knit 60 sts evenly around—15 sts in each quadrant. [Knit 1 rnd, purl 1 rnd] 3 times.

BO loosely.

Cut yarn and weave in all ends.

Lacy Cape

materials and tools

Artyarns Cashmere 1 (100% cashmere; 1.76oz/50g = 510yd/466m): (A), 1 skein, color # H11—approx 510yd/466m of lace weight yarn (0)

Artyarns Beaded Silk Light (100% silk w/glass beads; 1.76oz/50g = 160yd/146m): (B), 1 skein, color # H11S—approx 160yd/146m of lightweight yarn (3)

Knitting needles: 4mm (size 6 U.S.) 16"/40cm circular or size to obtain gauge

Stitch markers

Tapestry needle

gauge

18 sts/24 rows = 4"/10cm in Vertical Body Stitch

Always take time to check your gauge.

special abbreviation

Cdd (center double decrease): Slip 2, knit 1, pass slipped stitches over.

sizes

Small (Medium, Large)

finished measurements

Neck Circumference 18 (21, 23)"/46 (53, 58)cm

Bottom Circumference 44 (49, 54)"/112 (124, 137)cm

This delicate piece is finished with a feminine ruffle edge. It is worked in the round and is completely seamless.

design by
Laura Zukaite

skill level
intermediate

pattern stitches

VERTICAL BODY STITCH (MULTIPLE OF 6 STS + 1)

Row 1 (RS): *K1, yo, k1, cdd, k1, yo; rep from * to last st, k1.

Row 2: Knit.

Rep these 2 rows for Vertical Body Stitch pattern.

1X1 RIB (MULTIPLE OF 2 STS)

Rnd 1: *K1, p1; rep from * around.

Rep this rnd for 1x1 Rib.

instructions

BOTTOM PANELS (MAKE 2)

Using 4mm (size 6 U.S.) needle and A, CO 39 (51, 63) sts. Work back and forth in rows.

NOTE: Slip the first and knit the last stitch of every row (edge stitches).

Row 1 (RS): Sl 1 (edge st), work first row of Vertical Body Stitch pattern, k1 (edge st).

Row 2 (WS): Sl 1 (edge st), work in Vertical Body Stitch pattern as established to last st, k1 (edge st).

Next Row (RS): Work in pattern as established to end of row, CO 2 sts—41 (53, 65) sts.

Rep last row 17 more times—75 (87, 99) sts.

NOTE: Once you add 6 sts on each side, join them into another pattern repeat.

JOIN BOTTOM PANELS

Once you have 2 bottom panels completed, slip the sts for both panels onto the same needle and join in a round as follows:

Rnd 1: **K1, *K1, yo, k1, cdd, k1, yo; rep from * to 2 sts before end of one panel, k2, place marker (pm), rep from ** once more—150 (174, 198) sts.

Rnd 2: *K2, purl to 2 sts before the side marker, k2, rep from * once more.

Repeat last 2 rounds for 2"/5cm.

Dec Rnd: *K2, yo, dec 1 st, continue in pattern as established to 4 sts before side marker, dec 1 st, yo, k2, rep from * once more—146 (170, 194) sts.

Rep Dec Rnd on every other rnd 9 (10, 12) more times—110 (130, 146) sts. Work in 1x1 rib for 3 rnds.

FINISHING

Weave in ends.

RUFFLE

With RS facing and B, pick up and knit 200 (240, 280) sts around the bottom opening.

Work in 1x1 Rib for 1 rnd.

Inc Rnd: *K1, yo, p1, yo, rep from * around—400 (480, 560) sts.

Work in 1x1 Rib for 2 rnds.

Rep Inc Rnd—800 (960, 1120) sts.

Work in 1x1 Rib for 4 rnds.

BO loosely in pattern.

Block the Cape.

A dainty, feminine piece that highlights the drape and sparkle of its yarn, this lovely collar takes the stress out of lace knitting. The most basic beginner mistake, dropping a stitch, is purposefully done to give the garment lace-like fabric. Working the edging on tighter needles allows the collar to hug the neck while the ruffles tumble gracefully.

design by
Brooke Nico

skill level
easy

Elizabethan Collar

materials and tools

Artyarns Beaded Pearl & Sequins (100% silk with glass beads & sequins; 1.76oz/50g = 80yd/73m): (A), 1 skein, color # 271S—approx 80yd/73m of medium weight yarn (4)

Artyarns Silk Pearl (100% silk; 1.76oz/50g = 170yd/155m): (B), 1 skein, color # 1020—approx 170/155m of lightweight yarn (3)

Knitting needles: 5mm (size 8 U.S.) 32"/80cm circular needle, 4mm (size 6 U.S.) 24"/60cm circular needle or size to obtain gauge

Tapestry needle

gauge

24 sts/32 rows = 4"/10cm over k2, p1 rib using smaller needle

Always take time to check your gauge.

special abbreviation

Sk2p: Slip next st, k2tog, pass slipped st over.

special technique

Knitted Cast-On: *Knit into first st on lefthand needle, draw up a loop and place it on lefthand needle in front of first st; repeat from * for number of sts required.

note

You must use the Knitted Cast-On to work this pattern.

finished measurements

48" x 4"/122cm x 10cm

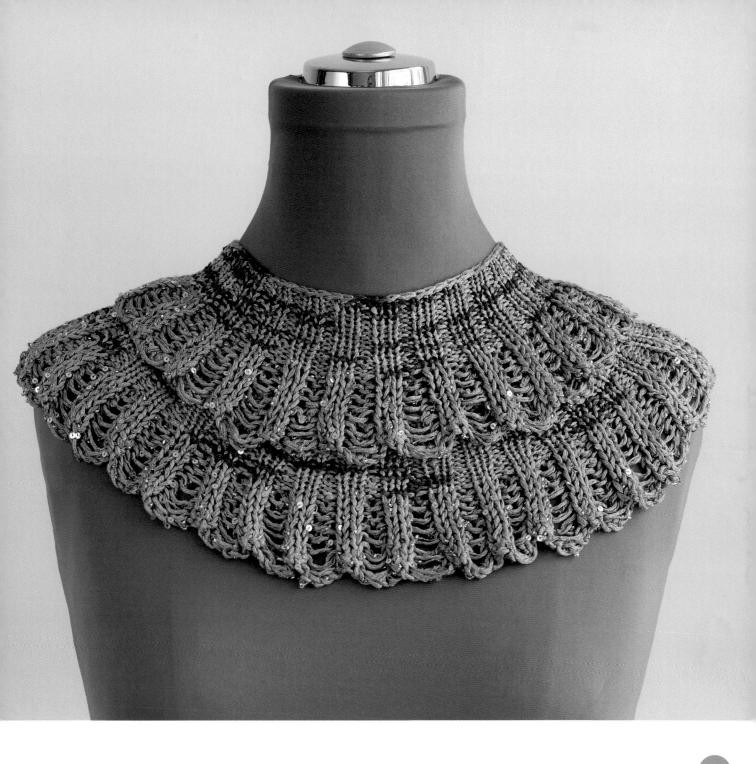

instructions

Using Knitted Cast-On with larger needle and A, CO 464 sts.

Row 1 (setup row): P2, *k1, sk2p, k1, p2, rep from * across—332 sts.

Row 2 (RS): K2, *p3, k2, rep from * across.

Row 3: P2, *k3, p2, rep from * across.

Rep rows 2 and 3 until piece measures 2"/5cm from CO, ending with row 3.

Next row: K2, *p1, drop next stitch off needle, p1, k2, rep from * across—266 sts.

Unravel all the dropped stitches down to cast-on row.

BEGIN RIBBING

Switch to smaller needle and B.

Row 1: P2, *k2, p2, rep from * across.

Row 2: K2, *p2, k2, rep from * across.

Row 3: Rep row 1.

Row 4: K2, *p2tog, k2, rep from * across—200 sts.

Row 5: P2, *k1, p2, rep from * across.

Row 6: K2, *p1, k2, rep from * across.

Rep Rows 5 and 6 for a total of 17 ribbing rows or desired height.

BO in rib pattern.

FINISHING

Weave in all ends. Block piece, fanning out dropped stitch edge.

Two-Color Sideways Garter Shawl

materials and tools

Artyarns Ensemble Glitter Light (50% cashmere, 50% silk; 2.82oz/80g = 400yd/366m): (A), 1 skein, color #1024S—approx 400yd/366m of lightweight yarn (3)

Artyarns Silk Essence (100% silk; 1.6oz/45g = 400yd/366m): (B), 1 skein, color #H1—approx 400yd/366m of lace weight yarn (1)

Knitting needles: 4.5mm (size 7 U.S.) or size to obtain gauge

Stitch markers

Tapestry needle

gauge

18sts/20rows = 4"/10cm in Garter Stitch with A

Always take time to check your gauge.

special abbreviations

w&t (wrap and turn): see page 124

ridge: A ridge consists of 2 rows and is referenced in the short row sections.

notes

This scarf is knitted side to side with the lace-patterned edging built right into the construction. Each time a bind-off-3-sts section of the edging is made, a rounded "tooth" is formed, which is the best way of keeping track of where you are in the pattern.

Making a yarn over at the beginning of the row can be a little tricky. Just drape the yarn over the empty needle and make sure you've wrapped the yarn around the needle before working the first purl stitch.

Every odd tooth is worked with A, and every even tooth (except Tooth 2 and Tooth 76) is worked with B, starting with Tooth 3. But the bind-off for each tooth is worked with both yarns held together.

Carry the unused yarn up alongside, twisting it around the working yarn, to make sure no unsightly loops are formed at the edges.

finished measurements

13½"/34cm deep x 62"/157cm long

This sideways knit garter stitch shawl uses short rows to shape it into a crescent that curves in a lovely way around the neck. The lace edging is built right in, and the neckline edging consists of pretty, delicate loops. The two colors alternate in separate "wedges."

design by
Iris Schreier

skill level
intermediate

instructions

With A, CO 4 sts.

TOOTH 1

Row 1: With A, k3, yo, p1—5 sts.

Row 2: Yo, p1, k to last 2 sts, yo, k2—7 sts.

Row 3: K2, [k1, p1, k1] in yo st, k to last 2 sts, yo, p2tog—9 sts.

Row 4: Yo, p1, yo, ssk, k to end—10 sts.

Row 5: Bind off 3 sts, k to last 2 sts, yo, p2tog—7 sts.

Row 6: Yo, p1, yo, ssk, k to last 2 sts, yo, k2—9 sts.

TOOTH 2 (INCREASE SECTION—3 STS INCREASED)

Row 1: With A, k2, [k1, p1, k1] in yo st, k to last 2 sts, yo, p2tog—11 sts.

Row 2: Yo, p1, yo, ssk, k to end—12 sts.

Row 3: K to last 2 sts, yo, p2tog—12 sts.

Row 4: Yo, p1, yo, ssk, k to end—13 sts.

Row 5: Bind off 3 sts, k to last 2 sts, yo, p2tog—10 sts.

Row 6: Yo, p1, yo, ssk, k to last 2 sts, yo, k2—12 sts.

TOOTH 3

Rep Tooth 2—15 sts.

TOOTH 4 (SHORT ROW SECTION)

Ridge 1: Attach B. With B, k2, [k1, p1, k1] in yo st, k1, w&t; k to end.

Ridge 2: K6, pick up wrap and k next st with its wrap, k1, w&t; k to end.

TOOTH 5 (INCREASE SECTION—3 STS INCREASED)

Inc Row 1: With A, k2, [k1, p1, k1] in yo st, k to marker, rm, pick up wrap and k next st with wrap, k to last 2 sts, yo, p2tog—17 sts.

Inc Row 2: Yo, p1, yo, ssk, k to end—18 sts.

Inc Row 3: K to last 2 sts, yo, p2tog.

Inc Row 4: Yo, p1, yo, ssk, k to end—19 sts.

Inc Row 5: Bind off 3 sts with A & B together, with B alone, k to last 2 sts, yo, p2tog—16 sts.

Inc Row 6: Yo, p1, yo, ssk, k to last 2 sts, yo, k2—18 sts.

TOOTH 6 (SHORT ROW SECTION)

Ridge 1: With B, k2, [k1, p1, k1] in yo st, k2, pm, w&t; k to end.

Ridge 2: K to marker, rm, pick up wrap and k next st with its wrap, k2, pm, w&t; k to end.

Ridge 3: Bind off 3 sts with A & B together, then with B, k to marker, rm, pick up wrap and k next st with wrap, k2, pm, w&t; k to last 2 sts, yo, k2.

TOOTH 7

Rep Tooth 5—21 sts.

TOOTH 8 (SHORT ROW SECTION)

Ridge 1: With B, k2, [k1, p1, k1] in yo st, k3, pm, w&t; k to end.

Ridge 2: K to marker, rm, pick up wrap and k next st with its wrap, k3, pm, w&t; k to end.

Ridge 3: Bind off 3 sts with A & B together, then with B, k to marker, rm, pick up wrap and k next st with wrap, k3, pm, w&t; k to last 2 sts, yo, k2.

TOOTH 9

Rep Tooth 5—24 sts.

TOOTH 10 (SHORT ROW SECTION)

Ridge 1: With B, k2, [k1, p1, k1] in yo st, k4, pm, w&t; k to end.

Ridge 2: K to marker, rm, pick up wrap and k next st with its wrap, k4, pm, w&t; k to end.

Ridge 3: Bind off 3 sts with A & B together, then with B, k to marker, rm, pick up wrap and k next st with wrap, k4, pm, w&t; k to last 2 sts, yo, k2.

TOOTH 11

Rep Tooth 5—27 sts.

TOOTH 12 (SHORT ROW SECTION)

Ridge 1: With B, k2, [k1, p1, k1] in yo st, k5, pm, w&t; k to end.

Ridge 2: K to marker, rm, pick up wrap and k next st with its wrap, k5, pm, w&t; k to end.

Ridge 3: Bind off 3 sts with A & B together, then with B, k to marker, rm, pick up wrap and k next st with wrap, k5, pm, w&t; k to last 2 sts, yo, k2.

TOOTH 13

Rep Tooth 5—30 sts.

TOOTH 14 (SHORT ROW SECTION)

Ridge 1: With B, k2, [k1, p1, k1] in yo st, k6, pm, w&t; k to end.

Ridge 2: K to marker, rm, pick up wrap and k next st with its wrap, k6, pm, w&t; k to end.

Ridge 3: Bind off 3 sts with A & B together, then with B, k to marker, rm, pick up wrap and k next st with wrap, k6, pm, w&t; k to last 2 sts, yo, k2.

TOOTH 15

Rep Tooth 5—33 sts.

TOOTH 16 (SHORT ROW SECTION)

Ridge 1: With B, k2, [k1, p1, k1] in yo st, k7, pm, w&t; k to end.

Ridge 2: K to marker, rm, pick up wrap and k next st with its wrap, k7, pm, w&t; k to end.

Ridge 3: Bind off 3 sts with A & B together, then with B, k to marker, rm, pick up wrap and k next st with wrap, k7, pm, w&t; k to last 2 sts, yo, k2.

TOOTH 17

Rep Tooth 5—36 sts.

TOOTH 18 (SHORT ROW SECTION)

Ridge 1: With B, k2, [k1, p1, k1] in yo st, k8, pm, w&t; k to end.

Ridge 2: K to marker, rm, pick up wrap and k next st with its wrap, k8, pm, w&t; k to end.

Ridge 3: Bind off 3 sts with A & B together, then with B, k to marker, rm, pick up wrap and k next st with wrap, k8, pm, w&t; k to last 2 sts, yo, k2—36 sts.

TOOTH 19

Rep Tooth 5—39 sts.

TOOTH 20 (SHORT ROW SECTION)

Ridge 1: With B, k2, [k1, p1, k1] in yo st, k9, pm, w&t; k to end.

Ridge 2: K to marker, rm, pick up wrap and k next st with its wrap, k9, pm, w&t; k to end.

Ridge 3: Bind off 3 sts with A & B together, then with B, k to marker, rm, pick up wrap and k next st with wrap, k9, pm, w&t; k to last 2 sts, yo, k2—39 sts.

TOOTH 21

Rep Tooth 5—42 sts.

TOOTH 22 (SHORT ROW SECTION)

Ridge 1: With B, k2, [k1, p1, k1] in yo st, k10, pm, w&t; k to end.

Ridge 2: K to marker, rm, pick up wrap and k next st with its wrap, k10, pm, w&t; k to end.

Ridge 3: Bind off 3 sts with A & B together, then with B, k to marker, rm, pick up wrap and k next st with wrap, k10, pm, w&t; k to last 2 sts, yo, k2—42 sts.

TOOTH 23 (DOUBLE INCREASE SECTION —6 STS INCREASED)

Inc Row 1: With A, k2, [k1, p1, k1] in yo st, k to marker, rm, pick up wrap and k next st with wrap, k to last 2 sts, yo, p2tog—44 sts.

Inc Row 2: Yo, p1, yo, ssk, k to last 2 sts, M1L, k to end—46 sts.

Inc Row 3: K to last 2 sts, yo, p2tog.

Inc Row 4: Yo, p1, yo, ssk, k to last 2 sts, M1L, k to end—48 sts.

Inc Row 5: Bind off 3 sts with A & B together, then with A, k to last 2 sts, yo, p2tog—45 sts.

Inc Row 6: Yo, p1, yo, ssk, k to last 2 sts, M1L, yo, k2—48 sts.

TOOTH 24 (SHORT ROW SECTION)

Ridge 1: With B, k2, [k1, p1, k1] in yo st, k13, pm, w&t; k to end.

Ridge 2: K to marker, rm, pick up wrap and k next st with its wrap, k13, pm, w&t; k to end.

Ridge 3: Bind off 3 sts with A & B together, then with B alone, k to marker, rm, pick up wrap and k next st with wrap, k13, pm, w&t; k to last 2 sts, yo, k2.

TOOTH 25

Rep Tooth 23—54 sts.

TOOTH 26 (SHORT ROW SECTION)

Ridge 1: With B, k2, [k1, p1, k1] in yo st, k15, pm, w&t; k to end.

Ridge 2: K to marker, rm, pick up wrap and k next st with its wrap, k15, pm, w&t; k to end.

Ridge 3: Bind off 3 sts with A & B together, then with B alone, k to marker, rm, pick up wrap and k next st with wrap, k15, pm, w&t; k to last 2 sts, yo, k2.

TOOTH 27

Rep Tooth 23—60 sts.

TOOTH 28 (SHORT ROW SECTION)

Ridge 1: With B, k2, [k1, p1, k1] in yo st, k17, pm, w&t; k to end.

Ridge 2: K to marker, rm, pick up wrap and k next st with its wrap, k17, pm, w&t; k to end.

Ridge 3: Bind off 3 sts with A & B together, then with B alone, k to marker, rm, pick up wrap and k next st with wrap, k17, pm, w&t; k to last 2 sts, yo, k2.

TOOTH 29

Rep Tooth 23—66 sts.

TOOTH 30 (SHORT ROW SECTION)

Ridge 1: With B, k2, [k1, p1, k1] in yo st, k19, pm, w&t; k to end.

Ridge 2: K to marker, rm, pick up wrap and k next st with its wrap, k19, pm, w&t; k to end.

Ridge 3: Bind off 3 sts with A & B together, then with B alone, k to marker, rm, pick up wrap and k next st with wrap, k19, pm, w&t; k to last 2 sts, yo, k2.

TOOTH 31

Rep Tooth 23—72 sts.

TOOTH 32 (SHORT ROW SECTION)

Ridge 1: With B, k2, [k1, p1, k1] in yo st, k21, pm, w&t; k to end.

Ridge 2: K to marker, rm, pick up wrap and k next st with its wrap, k21, pm, w&t; k to end.

Ridge 3: Bind off 3 sts with A & B together, then with B alone, k to marker, rm, pick up wrap and k next st with wrap, k21, pm, w&t; k to last 2 sts, yo, k2.

TOOTH 33

Rep Tooth 23—78 sts.

TOOTH 34 (SHORT ROW SECTION)

Ridge 1: With B, k2, [k1, p1, k1] in yo st, k23, pm, w&t; k to end.

Ridge 2: K to marker, rm, pick up wrap and k next st with its wrap, k23, pm, w&t; k to end.

Ridge 3: Bind off 3 sts with A & B together, then with B alone, k to marker, rm, pick up wrap and k next st with wrap, k23, pm, w&t; k to last 2 sts, yo, k2.

TOOTH 35 (WORK EVEN SECTION)

W-E Row 1: With A, k2, [k1, p1, k1] in yo st, k to marker, rm, pick up wrap and k next st with wrap, k to last 2 sts, yo, p2tog—80 sts.

W-E Row 2: Yo, p1, yo, ssk, k to last 7 sts, ssk, k5.

W-E Row 3: K to last 2 sts, yo, p2tog.

W-E Row 4: Yo, p1, yo, ssk, k to last 7 sts, ssk, k5.

W-E Row 5: Bind off 3 sts with A & B held together, then with A alone, k to last 2 sts, yo, p2tog—77 sts.

W-E Row 6: Yo, p1, yo, ssk, k to last 4 sts, ssk, yo, k2—78 sts.

TOOTH 36 (SHORT ROW SECTION)

Ridge 1: With B, k2, [k1, p1, k1] in yo st, k22, pm, w&t; k to end.

Ridge 2: K to marker, rm, pick up wrap and k next st with its wrap, k9, pm, w&t; k to end.

Ridge 3: Bind off 3 sts with A & B held together, then with B alone, k to marker, rm, pick up wrap and k next st with wrap, k9, pm, w&t; k to last 2 sts, yo, k2.

TEETH 37, 39, 41, 43

Rep Tooth 35.

TEETH 38, 40, 42, 44

Rep Tooth 36.

TOOTH 45 (DOUBLE DECREASE SECTION —6 STS DECREASED)

Dec Row 1: With A, k2, [k1, p1, k1] in yo st, k to marker, rm, pick up wrap and k next st with wrap, k to last 2 sts, yo, p2tog—80 sts.

Dec Row 2: Yo, p1, yo, ssk, k to last 10 sts, ssk, sssk, k5—78 sts.

Dec Row 3: K to last 2 sts, yo, p2tog.

Dec Row 4: Yo, p1, yo, ssk, k to last 10 sts, ssk, sssk, k5—76 sts.

Dec Row 5: Bind off 3 sts with A & B together, then with only A, k to last 2 sts, yo, p2tog—73 sts.

Dec Row 6: Yo, p1, yo, ssk, k to last 7 sts, ssk, sssk, yo, k2—72 sts.

TOOTH 46 (SHORT ROW SECTION)

Ridge 1: With B, k2, [k1, p1, k1] in yo st, k21, pm, w&t; k to end.

Ridge 2: K to marker, rm, pick up wrap and k next st with its wrap, k21, pm, w&t; k to end.

Ridge 3: Bind off 3 sts with A & B together, then with only B, k to marker, rm, pick up wrap and k next st with wrap, k21, pm, w&t; k to last 2 sts, yo, k2.

TOOTH 47

Rep Tooth 45—66 sts.

TOOTH 48 (SHORT ROW SECTION)

Ridge 1: With B, k2, [k1, p1, k1] in yo st, k19, pm, w&t; k to end.

Ridge 2: K to marker, rm, pick up wrap and k next st with its wrap, k19, pm, w&t; k to end.

Ridge 3: Bind off 3 sts with A & B together, then with only B, k to marker, rm, pick up wrap and k next st with wrap, k19, pm, w&t; k to last 2 sts, yo, k2.

TOOTH 49
Rep Tooth 45—60 sts.

TOOTH 50 (SHORT ROW SECTION)

Ridge 1: With B, k2, [k1, p1, k1] in yo st, k17, pm, w&t; k to end.

Ridge 2: K to marker, rm, pick up wrap and k next st with its wrap, k17, pm, w&t; k to end.

Ridge 3: Bind off 3 sts with A & B together, then with only B, k to marker, rm, pick up wrap and k next st with wrap, k17, pm, w&t; k to last 2 sts, yo, k2.

TOOTH 51
Rep Tooth 45—54 sts.

TOOTH 52 (SHORT ROW SECTION)

Ridge 1: With B, k2, [k1, p1, k1] in yo st, k15, pm, w&t; k to end.

Ridge 2: K to marker, rm, pick up wrap and k next st with its wrap, k15, pm, w&t; k to end.

Ridge 3: Bind off 3 sts with A & B together, then with only B, k to marker, rm, pick up wrap and k next st with wrap, k15, pm, w&t; k to last 2 sts, yo, k2.

TOOTH 53
Rep Tooth 45—48 sts.

TOOTH 54 (SHORT ROW SECTION)

Ridge 1: With B, k2, [k1, p1, k1] in yo st, k13, pm, w&t; k to end.

Ridge 2: K to marker, rm, pick up wrap and k next st with its wrap, k13, pm, w&t; k to end.

Ridge 3: Bind off 3 sts with A & B together, then with only B, k to marker, rm, pick up wrap and k next st with wrap, k13, pm, w&t; k to last 2 sts, yo, k2.

TOOTH 55

Rep Tooth 45—42 sts.

TOOTH 56 (SHORT ROW SECTION)

Ridge 1: With B, k2, [k1, p1, k1] in yo st, k11, pm, w&t; k to end.

Ridge 2: K to marker, rm, pick up wrap and k next st with its wrap, k11, pm, w&t; k to end.

Ridge 3: Bind off 3 sts with A & B together, then with only B, k to marker, rm, pick up wrap and k next st with wrap, k11, pm, w&t; k to last 2 sts, yo, k2.

TOOTH 57 (DECREASE SECTION—3 STS DECREASED)

Dec Row 1: With A, k2, [k1, p1, k1] in yo st, k to marker, rm, pick up wrap and k next st with wrap, k to last 2 sts, yo, p2tog—44 sts.

Dec Row 2: Yo, p1, yo, ssk, k to last 8 st, sssk, k5—43 sts.

Dec Row 3: K to last 2 sts, yo, p2tog.

Dec Row 4: Yo, p1, yo, ssk, k to last 8 sts, sssk, k5—42 sts.

Dec Row 5: Bind off 3 sts with A & B together, then with only A, k to last 2 sts, yo, p2tog—39 sts.

Dec Row 6: Yo, p1, yo, ssk, k to last 5 sts, sssk, yo, k2—39 sts.

TOOTH 58

Rep Tooth 22.

TOOTH 59

Rep Tooth 57—36 sts.

TOOTH 60

Rep Tooth 20.

TOOTH 61

Rep Tooth 57—33 sts.

TOOTH 62

Rep Tooth 18.

TOOTH 63

Rep Tooth 57—30 sts.

TOOTH 64

Rep Tooth 16.

TOOTH 65

Rep Tooth 57—27 sts.

TOOTH 66

Rep Tooth 14.

TOOTH 67

Rep Tooth 57—24 sts.

TOOTH 68

Rep Tooth 12.

TOOTH 69

Rep Tooth 57—21 sts.

TOOTH 70

Rep Tooth 10.

TOOTH 71

Rep Tooth 57—18 sts.

TOOTH 72

Rep Tooth 8.

TOOTH 73

Rep Tooth 57—15 sts.

TOOTH 74

Rep Tooth 6.

Cut B.

TOOTH 75 (DECREASE SECTION—3 STS DECREASED)

Dec Row 1: With A, k2, [k1, p1, k1] in yo st, k to marker, rm, pick up wrap and k next st with wrap, k to last 2 sts, yo, p2tog—17 sts.

Dec Row 2: Yo, p1, yo, ssk, k to last 8 st, sssk, k5—16 sts.

Dec Row 3: K to last 2 sts, yo, p2tog.

Dec Row 4: Yo, p1, yo, ssk, k to last 8 sts, sssk, k5—15 sts.

Dec Row 5: Bind off 3 sts, k to last 2 sts, yo, p2tog—12 sts.

Dec Row 6: Yo, p1, yo, ssk, k to last 5 sts, sssk, yo, k2—12 sts.

TOOTH 76 (DECREASE SECTION—3 STS DECREASED)

Dec Row 1: With A, k2, [k1, p1, k1] in yo st, k to last 2 sts, yo, p2tog—14 sts.

Dec Row 2: Yo, p1, yo, ssk, k3, sssk, k5—13 sts.

Dec Row 3: K to last 2 sts, yo, p2tog.

Dec Row 4: Yo, p1, yo, ssk, k2, sssk, k5—12 sts.

Dec Row 5: Bind off 3 sts, k to last 2 sts, yo, p2tog—9 sts.

Dec Row 6: Yo, p1, yo, ssk, k1, sssk, yo, k2—9 sts.

TOOTH 77

Dec Row 1: With A, k2, [k1, p1, k1] in yo st, k4, yo, p2tog—11 sts.

Dec Row 2: Yo, p1, yo, ssk, sssk, k5—10 sts.

Dec Row 3: K to last 2 sts, yo, p2tog.

Dec Row 4: Yo, p1, yo, ssk, sssk, k4—9 sts.

Dec Row 5: Bind off 3 sts, k3, yo, p2tog—6 sts.

Dec Row 6: Yo, p1, yo, ssk, sssk—5 sts.

Bind off all sts.

FINISHING

Weave in ends. Wet-block and pin to desired measurements. Let dry before moving.

Vineyard Shawl

materials and tools

Artyarns Beaded Pearl & Sequins (100% silk w/ glass beads & sequins; 1.76oz/50g = 80yd/73m): (A), 1 skein, color # 1010S—approx 80yd/73m of medium weight yarn (4)

Artyarns Silk Pearl (100% silk, 1.76oz/50g = 170yd/155m): (B), 1 skein, color 1010—approx 170yd/155m of lightweight yarn (3)

Knitting needles: 5.5mm (size 9 U.S.) 24"/60cm or longer circular needle or size to obtain gauge

Stitch marker

Cable needle

Tapestry needle

gauge

13½ sts/16 rows = 4"/10cm in Step 2 Lace Pattern Stitch

Always take time to check your gauge.

special abbreviation

c6L: Slip 3 sts to cable needle and hold in front, k3, then k3 from cable needle.

special technique

Knitted Cast-On: *Knit into first st on lefthand needle, draw up a loop and place it on lefthand needle in front of first st; repeat from * for number of sts required.

Turn: Switch needles so that your right needle becomes your left and your left needle becomes your right, so that you can continue to work in the opposite direction.

note

Edging is worked sideways with Yarn A, then stitches are picked up and purled with Yarn A. Yarn is cut. Yarn B will be attached, and the rest of the shawl will be knitted with B sideways, joining every other row to the edging.

finished measurements

12"/30cm at deepest point and 56"/142cm from tip to tip

This shawl evokes a lattice fence that could be used to keep vineyard plants upright. Its airy, openwork design maximizes the yardage of two small skeins of yarn. The cable panel adds substance and nice contrast to the gossamer lace portion.

design by
Iris Schreier

skill level
intermediate

instructions

STEP 1: EDGING

CO 9 sts with A.

Row 1: K1tbl, k4, [yo, k2tog] 2 times.

Rows 2, 4, 6, 8: Using Knitted Cast-on, make 1 st, p to last st, sl1 wyif.

Row 3: K1tbl, k3, [yo, k2tog] 3 times—10 sts.

Row 5: K1tbl, k2, [yo, k2tog] 4 times —11 sts.

Row 7: K1tbl, k1, [yo, k2tog] 5 times— 12 sts.

Row 9: K1tbl, k10, k2tog—12 sts.

Rows 10, 12, 14, 16, 18: K1, p to last st, sl1wyif.

Row 11: K1tbl, k1, [yo, k2tog] 5 times.

Row 13: K1tbl, k1, [k2tog, yo] 4 times, k2tog—11 sts.

Row 15: K1tbl, k2, [k2tog, yo] 3 times, k2tog—10 sts.

Row 17: K1tbl, k3, [k2tog, yo] 2 times, k2tog—9 sts.

Row 19: K1tbl, k4, k2tog, yo, k2tog— 8 sts.

Row 20: Using knitted cast-on, make 1 st, p to last st, sl1 wyif.

Repeat Rows 1–20 nine more times, for a total of 10 repeats.

Using A, pick up and purl 100 sts across slipped edge. Cut A.

STEP 2

You will be working sideways, joining to the Step 1 edging with an ssk at the end of each RS row.

Attach B and using Knitted Cast-On, CO 12 sts, adding them to the top-most of the 100 sts on the needle— 112 sts.

Row 1: K1, k2tog, yo2, ssk, place marker (pm), c6L, ssk, turn.

Row 2 and all even rows: Sl1p, p to last st, working [k1, p1] in all yo2 st from previous row, and slipping marker, k1.

Rows 3: K1, k2tog, yo2, ssk, k to marker, yo, slip marker (sm), k6, ssk, turn—1 st increased.

Rows 5–9: K1, k2tog, yo2, ssk, k to marker, yo, sm, k6, ssk, turn—1 st increased each RS row, for a total of 3 sts increased.

Row 11: K1, [k2tog, yo2, ssk] 2 times, sm, c6L, ssk, turn—no sts increased.

Rows 13–19: K1, [k2tog, yo2, ssk] 2 times, k to marker, yo, sm, k6, ssk, turn—1 st increased each RS row, for a total of 4 sts increased.

Row 21: K1, [k2tog, yo2, ssk] 3 times, sm, c6L, ssk, turn.

Rows 23–29: K1, [k2tog, yo2, ssk] 3 times, k to marker, yo, sm, k6, ssk, turn—1 st increased each RS row, for a total of 4 sts increased.

Row 31: K1, [k2tog, yo2, ssk] 4 times, sm, c6L, ssk, turn.

Rows 33–39: K1, [k2tog, yo2, ssk] 4 times, k to marker, yo, sm, k6, ssk, turn—1 st increased each RS row, for a total of 4 sts increased.

Row 41: K1, [k2tog, yo2, ssk] 5 times, sm, c6L, ssk, turn.

Rows 43–49: K1, [k2tog, yo2, ssk] 5 times, k to marker, yo, sm, k6, ssk, turn—1 st increased each RS row, for a total of 4 sts increased.

Row 51: K1, [k2tog, yo2, ssk] 6 times, sm, c6L, ssk, turn.

Rows 53–59: K1, [k2tog, yo2, ssk] 6 times, k to marker, yo, sm, k6, ssk, turn—1 st increased each RS row, for a total of 4 sts increased.

Row 61: K1, [k2tog, yo2, ssk] 7 times, sm, c6L, ssk, turn.

Rows 63–69: K1, [k2tog, yo2, ssk] 7 times, k to marker, yo, sm, k6, ssk, turn—1 st increased each RS row, for a total of 4 sts increased.

Row 71: K1, [k2tog, yo2, ssk] 8 times, sm, c6L, ssk, turn.

Rows 73–79: K1, [k2tog, yo2, ssk] 8 times, sm, k6, ssk, turn—no sts increased.

Rows 80–130: Repeat rows 71–80 five times—no sts increased or decreased.

Row 131: K1, [k2tog, yo2, ssk] 7 times, k2, k2tog, c6L, ssk, turn—1 st decreased.

Row 133: K1, [k2tog, yo2, ssk] 7 times, k1, k2tog, k6, ssk, turn— 1 st decreased.

Row 135: K1, [k2tog, yo2, ssk] 7 times, k2tog, k6, ssk, turn—1 st decreased.

Row 137: K1, [k2tog, yo2, ssk] 6 times, k2tog, yo2, cdd, k6, ssk, turn—1 st decreased.

Row 139: K1, [k2tog, yo2, ssk] 7 times, k6, ssk, turn—no sts decreased.

Row 141: K1, [k2tog, yo2, ssk] 6 times, k2, k2tog, c6L, ssk, turn—1 st decreased.

Row 143: K1, [k2tog, yo2, ssk] 6 times, k1, k2tog, k6, ssk, turn— 1 st decreased.

Row 145: K1, [k2tog, yo2, ssk] 6 times, k2tog, k6, ssk, turn—1 st decreased.

Row 147: K1, [k2tog, yo2, ssk] 5 times, k2tog, yo2, cdd, k6, ssk, turn—1 st decreased.

Row 149: K1, [k2tog, yo2, ssk] 6 times, k6, ssk, turn—no sts decreased.

Row 151: K1, [k2tog, yo2, ssk] 5 times, k2, k2tog, c6L, ssk, turn—1 st decreased.

Row 153: K1, [k2tog, yo2, ssk] 5 times, k1, k2tog, k6, ssk, turn—1 st decreased.

Row 155: K1, [k2tog, yo2, ssk] 5 times, k2tog, k6, ssk, turn—1 st decreased.

Row 157: K1, [k2tog, yo2, ssk] 4 times, k2tog, yo2, cdd, k6, ssk, turn—1 st decreased.

Row 159: K1, [k2tog, yo2, ssk] 5 times, k6, ssk, turn—no sts decreased.

Row 161: K1, [k2tog, yo2, ssk] 4 times, k2, k2tog, c6L, ssk, turn—1 st decreased.

Row 163: K1, [k2tog, yo2, ssk] 4 times, k1, k2tog, k6, ssk, turn—1 st decreased.

Row 165: K1, [k2tog, yo2, ssk] 4 times, k2tog, k6, ssk, turn—1 st decreased.

Row 167: K1, [k2tog, yo2, ssk] 3 times, k2tog, yo2, cdd, k6, ssk, turn—1 st decreased.

Row 169: K1, [k2tog, yo2, ssk] 4 times, k6, ssk, turn—no sts decreased.

Row 171: K1, [k2tog, yo2, ssk] 3 times, k2, k2tog, c6L, ssk, turn—1 st decreased.

Row 173: K1, [k2tog, yo2, ssk] 3 times, k1, k2tog, k6, ssk, turn—1 st decreased.

edging chart

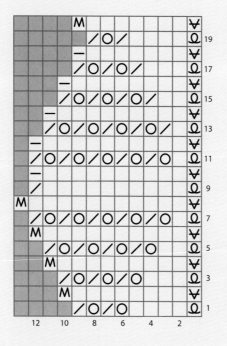

12 10 8 6 4 2

	c6l
O	yo
∧	cdd
☐	knit on RS, purl on WS
Ω	k1 tbl
/	k2tog
M	m1
⋎	sl wyif
\	ssk
▨	no stitch
−	knit on WS

Row 175: K1, [k2tog, yo2, ssk] 3 times, k2tog, k6, ssk, turn—1 st decreased.

Row 177: K1, [k2tog, yo2, ssk] 2 times, k2tog, yo2, cdd, k6, ssk, turn—1 st decreased.

Row 179: K1, [k2tog, yo2, ssk] 3 times, k6, ssk, turn—no sts decreased.

Row 181: K1, [k2tog, yo2, ssk] 2 times, k2, k2tog, c6L, ssk, turn—1 st decreased.

Row 183: K1, [k2tog, yo2, ssk] 2 times, k1, k2tog, k6, ssk, turn—1 st decreased.

Row 185: K1, [k2tog, yo2, ssk] 2 times, k2tog, k6, ssk, turn—1 st decreased.

Row 187: K1, k2tog, yo2, ssk, k2tog, yo2, cdd, k6, ssk, turn—1 st decreased.

Row 189: K1, [k2tog, yo2, ssk] 2 times, k6, ssk, turn—no sts decreased.

Row 191: K1, k2tog, yo2, ssk, k2, k2tog, c6L, ssk, turn—1 st decreased.

Row 193: K1, k2tog, yo2, ssk, k1, k2tog, k6, ssk, turn—1 st decreased.

Row 195: K1, k2tog, yo2, ssk, k2tog, k6, ssk, turn—1 st decreased.

Row 197: K1, [k2tog, yo2, cdd], k6, ssk, turn.

Row 199: K1, [k2tog, yo2, ssk], k6, ssk, turn.

Row 200: S1p, p to last st, working [k1, p1] in all yo2 st from previous row, and removing marker, k1.

FINISHING

Bind off remaining sts loosely. Cut yarn, weave in ends.

Wrapped Scarf

materials and tools

Artyarns Ensemble 4 (50% silk, 50% cashmere; 2.82oz/80g = 200yd/ 183m): (A), 1 skein, color #H13; (B), 1 skein, color #H23—approx 400yd/366m of medium weight yarn (4)

Knitting needles: 5mm (size 8 U.S.) 36"/90cm circular needle or size to obtain gauge

Crochet hook

gauge

13 sts/24 rows = 4"/10cm in Stockinette Stitch

Always take time to check your gauge.

special abbreviations

Cdd (center double decrease): Slip 2, knit 1, pass slipped stitches over.

Kfb: Knit in front and back of same stitch.

notes

1. This scarf is knitted top down in two parts. Part 1 is in color A. Part 2 is entirely in color B.

2. Work back and forth in rows on circular needle as if working with straight needles.

finished measurements

6"/15cm wide x 82"/208cm long, blocked

Designed to wrap around and around, this scarf has an interesting construction. You build the width with short rows at the edges, right at the beginning, to make it wider and shallower than a standard top-down scarf. Then a lovely lace pattern enhances the shape.

design by
Iris Schreier

skill level
intermediate

instructions

PART 1

Knitted entirely with A.

CO 4 sts.

Row 1 (RS): [Kfb, yo, k1, turn; sl1, k3] 3 times—6 sts increased.

Row 2 (RS): Kfb, yo, k8, yo, k1—3 sts increased.

Row 3 (WS): [Kfb, k2, turn; sl1, k2, yo, k1] 3 times—6 sts increased.

Row 4: Kfb, k to end—1 st increased.

Repeat rows 1–4 seven more times for a total of 132 sts.

Next Row (RS): [Kfb, yo, k1, turn; sl1, k3] 2 times—4 sts increased.

Next Row (RS): Kfb, yo, k8, yo, k1—3 sts increased.

Next Row (WS): [Kfb, k2, turn; sl1, k2, yo, k1] 2 times—4 sts increased.

Next Row: Kfb, k to last st, kfb—2 sts increased—145 sts.

Chart 1 (see chart at right)—repeat section between red lines 11 times.

Work written instructions for chart 1 lace pattern as follows:

Row 1: K4, k2tog, yo, k1, [yo, ssk, k7, k2tog, yo, k1] 11 times, yo, ssk, k4.

Row 2: K1, p4, yo, [p3, yo, p9, yo] 11 times, p3, yo, p4, k1.

Row 3: K3, k2tog, yo, k2tog, yo, k1, yo, [ssk, yo, ssk, k5, k2tog, yo, k2tog, yo, k1, yo] 11 times, ssk, yo, ssk, k3.

Row 4: K1, p3, yo, p1, [p6, yo, p7, yo, p1] 11 times, p6, yo, p3, k1.

Row 5: K2, [k2tog, yo] twice, [k2tog, yo, k1, (yo, ssk) 3 times, k3, (k2tog, yo) 3 times, k1, yo, ssk] 11 times, [yo, ssk] twice, k2.

pattern chart 1

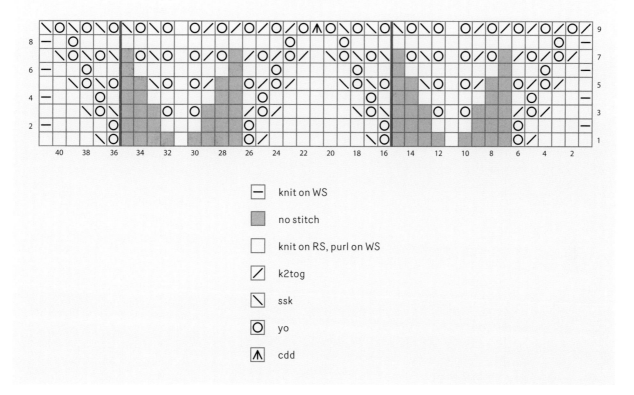

- — knit on WS
- � no stitch

Symbol	Meaning
—	knit on WS
(gray)	no stitch
(blank)	knit on RS, purl on WS
/	k2tog
\	ssk
O	yo
∧	cdd

Row 6: K1, p2, yo, p2, [p9, yo, p5, yo, p2] 11 times, p9, yo, p2, k1.

Row 7: K1, [k2tog, yo] 4 times, k1, yo, ssk, yo, [(ssk, yo) twice, ssk, k1, (k2tog, yo) 4 times, k1, yo, ssk, yo] 11 times, [ssk, yo] twice, ssk, k1.

Row 8: K1, p1, yo, p3, [p12, yo, p3, yo, p3] 11 times, p12, yo, p1, k1.

Row 9: [K2tog, yo] 5 times, k1, [yo, ssk] twice, [(yo, ssk) twice, yo, cdd, (yo, k2tog) 4 times, yo, k1, (yo, ssk) twice] 11 times, [yo, ssk] 3 times.

Row 10: K1, p to last st, k1.
Bind off all 241 sts loosely. Cut yarn.

PART 2

Knitted entirely with B.

With B and right side facing, pick up and knit 241 sts in the backs of the bound off sts (see page 122, Picking Up Stitches with Decorative Edge Showing). Kfb, p to last st, kfb—243 sts.

Chart 2 (see chart on page 110)—repeat section between red lines 11 times.

Row 1: K1, yo, k1, yo, ssk, k8, [k7, k2tog, yo, k1, yo, ssk, k8] 11 times, k7, k2tog, yo, k1, yo, k1.

Row 2: K1, yo, p3, yo, p8, [p9, yo, p3, yo, p8] 11 times, p9, yo, p3, yo, k1.

Row 3: K1, yo, k2tog, yo, k1, [yo, ssk] twice, k7, [k6, (k2tog, yo) twice, k1, (yo, ssk) twice, k7] 11 times, k6, [k2tog, yo] twice, k1, yo, ssk, yo k1.

Row 4: K1, yo, p7, yo, p7, [p8, yo, p7, yo, p7] 11 times, p8, yo, p7, yo, k1.

Row 5: K1, yo, [k2tog, yo] twice, k1, [yo, ssk] 3 times, k6, [k5, (k2tog, yo) 3 times, k1, (yo, ssk) 3 times, k6] 11 times, k5, (k2tog, yo) 3 times, k1, (yo, ssk) twice, yo, k1.

Row 6: K1, yo, p11, yo, p6, [p7, yo, p11, yo, p6] 11 times, p7, yo, p11, yo, k1.

Row 7: K1, yo, [k2tog, yo] 3 times, k1, [yo, ssk] 4 times, k5, [k4, (k2tog, yo) 4 times, k1, (yo, ssk) 4 times, k5] 11 times, k4, [k2tog, yo] 4 times, k1, [yo, ssk] 3 times, yo, k1.

Row 8: K1, p to last st, k1.

Bind off loosely using Stretchy Bind-Off method (see page 123).

FINISHING

Weave in ends.

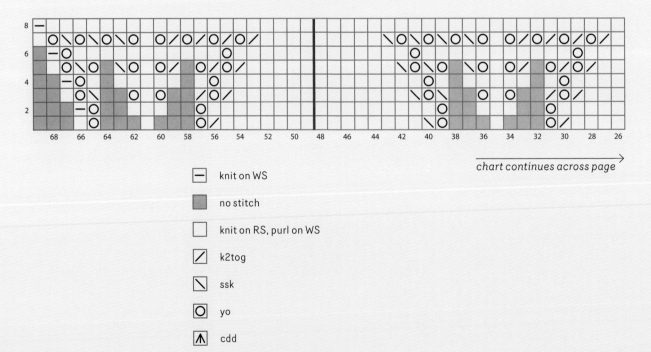

pattern chart 2

chart continues across page →

| — | knit on WS |
| no stitch |
| knit on RS, purl on WS |
/	k2tog
\	ssk
O	yo
Λ	cdd

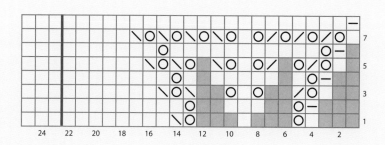

																									—
					\	O	\	O	\	O	\	O			O	/	O	/	O	/	O	/			7
							O			O											O		O		—	
					\	O	\	O		\		O		\		O	/		O	/	O	/	O		5
							O		▓		▓								O		O		—		
					\	O	\	O	▓		▓		O			O			/	O	/	O			3
							O		▓		▓								/		O		—		
					\	O	\	O	▓		▓						O			O					1

24   22   20   18   16   14   12   10   8   6   4   2

Build this shallow triangle scarf quite easily from the top down, alternating stockinette and garter panels. To make things interesting, I've added an optional perpendicular detail that creates a striking balance to the long lines formed by the stripes. The perpendicular lines can slowly grow to make a deep triangle (as shown in the blue and variegated red/teal version of the scarf) or remain one size to maintain the shape of the shallow triangle (as shown in the blue and yellow version)—instructions are given for both options.

design by
Iris Schreier

skill level
intermediate

Egyptian Scarf

materials and tools

Large Version (Variegated Red/Teal):

Artyarns Ensemble Light (50% silk, 50% cashmere; 2.82oz/80g = 400yd/366m): (A), 1 skein, color # H26S; (B), 1 skein, color #1026— approx 800yd/732m of lightweight yarn (3)

Small Version (Blue and Yellow):

Artyarns Cashmere Sock Yarn (67% cashmere, 25% wool, 8% nylon; 1.76oz/50g = 160yd/146m): (A), 1 skein, color # 320; (B) 1 skein, color # 924—approx 320yd/292m of fine yarn (2)

Knitting needles: 5mm (size 8 U.S.) 24–32"/60–80cm circular needle or size to obtain gauge

Stitch marker

Tapestry needle

gauge

18 sts/24 rows = 4"/10cm in Stockinette Stitch.

Always take time to check your gauge.

special abbreviations

Cdd (center double decrease): Slip 2, knit 1, pass slipped stitches over.

Kfb: Knit in front and back of same stitch.

Kfbf: Knit in front, back, and front again of same stitch.

Pfb: Purl in front and back of same stitch.

special techniques

Knitted Cast-On: *Knit into first st on LH needle, draw up a loop and place it on LH needle in front of first st; rep from * for number of sts required.

Turn: Switch needles so that your right needle becomes your left and your left needle becomes your right so that you can continue to work in the opposite direction.

finished measurements

Large: 57"/145cm long and 20"/51cm wide at center of triangle

Small: 51"/130cm long and 14½"/37cm wide at center of triangle

instructions

PART 1

Work back and forth in rows on circular needle.

FIRST STRIPED SECTION

With A, CO 3 sts.

Row 1: Kfb, kfb, place marker (pm), kfb—6 sts.

Row 2: Kfb, p to marker, remove marker (rm), pfb, pm, p to last st, kfb—9 sts.

Row 3: Kfbf, k to marker, rm, kfb, pm, k to last st, kfb—13 sts.

Row 4: Kfb, p to marker, rm, pfb, pm, p to last st, kfb—16 sts.

Attach B. With B.

Row 5: Kfbf, k to marker, rm, kfb, pm, k to last st, kfbf—21 sts.

Row 6: Kfb, k to marker, rm, kfb, pm, k to last st, kfb—24 sts.

Carry A up along side, knitting with both A and B in the first part of the first kfb. *Refer to this blog post for a photo tutorial: http://www.artyarns.com/cleopatra-shawl-knitalong/.*

Rows 7-10: Rep rows 5 and 6 twice—40 sts.

SECOND STRIPED SECTION

Carry B up along side, knitting with both A and B in the first part of the first kfbf.

Rows 11-16: Rep Rows 3 and 4 three times—64 sts.

Rows 17-22: Rep Rows 5 and 6 three times—88 sts.

NEXT 1 (2) STRIPED SECTION(S)

Rep Second Striped Section 1 (2) time(s)—136 (184) sts.

PART 2 (WORK SIDEWAYS IN ROWS)

Small Version Only

RIGHT SIDE PERPENDICULAR STRIPES

NOTE: You will switch colors every 3 rows. Make sure to carry the unworked yarn up and twist it around the working yarn to prevent unsightly loops from forming.

Cut A. With B, using Knitted Cast-On, CO 3 sts.

Row 1: With B, k2, p2tog, turn; sl1p, k1, sl1p, turn.

Rows 2 and 3: With B, k1tbl, k1, p2tog, turn; sl1p, k1, sl1p, turn.

Attach A. Make sure to twist B (the yarn not being worked) around A to carry it along without unsightly loops.

Rows 4-6: With A, k1tbl, k1, p2tog, turn; sl1p, p1, sl1p, turn.

Make sure to twist A (the yarn not being worked) around B to carry it along without unsightly loops.

Rows 7-9: With B, k1tbl, k1, p2tog, turn; sl1p, k1, sl1p, turn.

Row 10: With A, k1tbl, k1, M1, p2tog, turn; sl1p, p2, sl1p, turn—increase of 1 st.

Rows 11 and 12: With A, k1tbl, k2, p2tog, turn; sl1p, p2, sl1p, turn.

Rows 13-15: With B, k1tbl, k2, p2tog, turn; sl1p, k2, sl1p, turn.

Row 16: With A, k1tbl, k2, M1, p2tog, turn; sl1p, p3, sl1p, turn—increase of 1 st.

Rows 17 and 18: With A, k1tbl, k3, p2tog, turn; sl1p, p3, sl1p, turn.

Rows 19-21: With B, k1tbl, k3, p2tog, turn; sl1p, k3, sl1p, turn.

Row 22: With A, k1tbl, k3, M1, p2tog, turn; sl1p, p4, sl1p, turn—increase of 1 st.

Rows 23 and 24: With A, k1tbl, k4, p2tog, turn; sl1p, p4, sl1p, turn.

Rows 25-27: With B, k1tbl, k4, p2tog, turn; sl1p, k4, sl1p, turn.

Rows 28-30: With A, k1tbl, k4, p2tog, turn; sl1p, p4, sl1p, turn.

Rows 31-33: With B, k1tbl, k4, p2tog, turn; sl1p, k4, sl1p, turn.

Rows 34-63: Repeat Rows 28-33 five times.

Rows 64-66: Rep Rows 28-30.

Rows 67 and 68: With B, k1tbl, k4, p2tog, turn; sl1p, k4, sl1p, turn.

Cut A and B, and slide to other end of needle to work perpendicular stripes on other side.

WRONG SIDE PERPENDICULAR STRIPES

With B, using Knitted Cast-On, cast on 3 sts.

Row 1: With B, k2, ssk. Turn.

Rows 2 and 3: With B, sl1p, k1, sl1p, turn; k1tbl, k1, ssk, turn.

Attach A. Make sure to twist B (the yarn not being worked) around A to carry it along without unsightly loops.

Rows 4–6: With A, sl1p, k1, sl1p, turn; k1tbl, p1, ssk, turn.

Make sure to twist A (the yarn not being worked) around B to carry it along without unsightly loops.

Rows 7–9: With B, sl1p, k1, sl1p, turn; k1tbl, k1, ssk, turn.

Row 10: With A, sl1p, k1, sl1p, turn; k1tbl, p1, M1, ssk, turn—increase of 1 st.

Rows 11 and 12: With A, sl1p, k2, sl1p, turn; k1tbl, p2, ssk, turn.

Rows 13–15: With B, sl1p, k2, sl1p, turn; k1tbl, k2, ssk, turn.

Row 16: With A, sl1p, k2, sl1p, turn; k1tbl, p2, M1, ssk, turn—increase of 1 st.

Rows 17 and 18: With A, sl1p, k3, sl1p, turn; k1tbl, p3, ssk, turn.

Rows 19–21: With B, sl1p, k3, sl1p, turn; k1tbl, k3, ssk, turn.

Row 22: With A, sl1p, k3, sl1p, turn; k1tbl, p3, M1, ssk, turn—increase of 1 st.

Rows 23 and 24: With A, sl1p, k4, sl1p, turn; k1tbl, p4, ssk, turn.

Rows 25–27: With B, sl1p, k4, sl1p, turn; k1tbl, k4, ssk, turn.

Rows 28–30: With A, sl1p, k4, sl1p, turn; k1tbl, p4, ssk, turn.

Rows 31–33: With B, sl1p, k4, sl1p, turn; k1tbl, k4, ssk, turn.

Rows 34–63: Repeat Rows 28–33 five times.

Rows 64–66: Rep Rows 28–30.

Rows 67 and 68: With B, sl1p, k4, sl1p, turn; k1tbl, k4, ssk, turn. Cut A and B.

Large Version Only

RIGHT SIDE PERPENDICULAR STRIPES

NOTE: You will switch colors every 3 rows—make sure to carry the unworked yarn up and twist it around the working yarn to prevent unsightly loops from forming.

Cut A. With B, using Knitted Cast-On, CO 4 sts.

Row 1: With B, k3, p2tog, turn; sl1p, k2, sl1p, turn.

Rows 2 and 3: With B, k1tbl, k2, p2tog, turn; sl1p, k2, sl1p, turn.

Attach A. Make sure to twist B (the yarn not being worked) around A to carry it along without unsightly loops.

Row 4: With A, k1tbl, k2, M1, p2tog, turn; sl1p, p3, sl1p, turn—increase of 1 st.

Rows 5 and 6: With A, k1tbl, k3, p2tog, turn; sl1p, p3, sl1p, turn.

Make sure to twist A (the yarn not being worked) around B to carry it along without unsightly loops.

Rows 7 and 8: With B, k1tbl, k3 , p2tog, turn; sl1p, k3, sl1p, turn.

Row 9: With B, k1tbl, k3, pm, p2tog, turn; sl1p, k3, sl1p, slipping marker, turn.

Row 10: With A, k1tbl, k to marker, M1, slip marker (sm), p2tog, turn; sl1p, p to last st, sl1p, turn—increase of 1 st.

Rows 11 and 12: With A, k1tbl, k to marker, sm, p2tog, turn; sl1p, p to last st, sl1p, turn.

Rows 13–15: With B, k1tbl, k to marker, sm, p2tog, turn; sl1p, k to last st, sl1p, turn.

Rows 16–87: Rep rows 10–15 twelve times.

Rows 88–92: Rep rows 10–14.

Cut A and B, and slide to other end of needle to work perpendicular stripes on other side.

WRONG SIDE PERPENDICULAR STRIPES

With B, using knitted cast on, CO 4 sts.

Row 1: With B, k3, ssk. Turn.

Rows 2 and 3: With B, sl1p, k2, sl1p, turn; k1tbl, k2, ssk, turn.

Attach A. Make sure to twist B (the yarn not being worked) around A to carry it along without unsightly loops.

Row 4: With A, sl1p, k2, sl1p, turn; k1tbl, p2, M1, ssk, turn—increase of 1 st.

Rows 5 and 6: With A, sl1p, k3, sl1p, turn; k1tbl, p3, ssk, turn.

Make sure to twist A (the yarn not being worked) around B to carry it along without unsightly loops.

Rows 7 and 8: With B, sl1p, k3, sl1p, turn; k1tbl, k3, ssk, turn.

Row 9: With B, sl1p, k3, sl1p, turn; k1tbl, k3, pm, ssk, turn.

Row 10: With A, sl1p, k to last st, sl1p, turn; k1tbl, p to marker, M1, sm, ssk, turn—increase of 1 st.

Rows 11 and 12: With A, sl1p, k to last st, sl1p, turn; k1tbl, p to marker, sm, ssk, turn.

Rows 13–15: With B, sl1p, k to last st, sl1p, turn; k1tbl, k to marker, sm, ssk, turn.

Rows 16–87: Rep rows 10–15 twelve times.

Rows 88–92: Rep rows 10–14.

Cut A and B.

CENTER DIAMOND

You will now fill in the center diamond as follows:

Since there are so few sts on the needle, it may be easier to switch to double pointed needles—that is up to you.

With RS facing, attach B to the top-most perpendicular on the right side (see diagram at right), and work as follows:

Small Version Only

Row 1: With B, k1tbl, k4, sl1p, pick up 1 st in center, k1, pass slipped and pick-up center st over the knit st, k4, sl1p, turn—11 sts.

Row 2: With B, k1tbl, k to last st, sl1p, turn.

Row 3: Attach A, and with A, k1tbl, k3, cdd, k3, sl1p, turn—9 sts.

Row 4: With A, k1tbl, p to last st, sl1p, turn.

Row 5: With A, k1tbl, k2, cdd, k2, sl1p, turn—7 sts.

Row 6: With A, k1tbl, p to last st, sl1p, turn.

Row 7: With A, k1tbl, k1, cdd, k1, sl1p, turn—5 sts.

Row 8: With A, k1tbl, p to last st, sl1p, turn.

Row 9: With A, k1tbl, cdd, sl1p, turn—3 sts.

Bind off all sts loosely. Cut A and B.

Large Version Only

Row 1: With B, k1tbl, k17, pm, sl1p, pick up 1 st in center, k1, pass slipped and pick-up center st over the knit st, k to last st, sl1p, turn—37 sts.

Row 2: With B, k1tbl, k to last st, slipping marker, sl1p, turn.

Row 3: Attach A, and with A, k1tbl, k to st before marker, transfer st from left to right needle to remove marker, then return st to left needle, pm, cdd, k to last st, sl1p, turn—35 sts.

Row 4: With A, k1tbl, p to last st, slipping marker, sl1p, turn.

Rows 5–8: Rep rows 3 and 4 twice—31 sts.

Row 9: With B, k1tbl, k to st before marker, transfer st from left to right needle to remove marker, then return st to left needle, pm, cdd, k to last st, sl1p—29 sts.

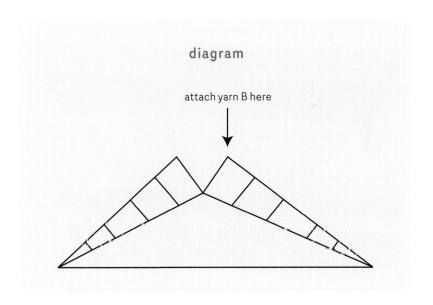

diagram

attach yarn B here

Row 10: With B: k1tbl, k to last st, slipping marker, sl1p, turn.

Rows 11–14: Rep rows 9 and 10 twice—25 sts.

Rows 15–20: Rep rows 3 and 4 three times—19 sts.

Rows 21–26: Rep rows 9 and 10 three times—13 sts.

Rows 27–32: Rep rows 3 and 4 three times—7 sts.

Rows 33–36: Rep rows 9 and 10 twice—3 sts.

Bind off all sts loosely. Cut A and B.

PART 3 (WORK BACK AND FORTH IN ROWS)

Small Version Only

With RS facing and B, pick up 74 sts on first half of triangle, pick up 1 st at center point, pm, and 74 sts on second half of triangle—149 sts total.

Set-up Row (WS): With B, kfb, k to marker, rm, kfb, pm, k to last st, kfb—152 sts.

Row 1: With B, kfbf, k to marker, rm, kfb, pm, k to last st, kfbf—157 sts.

Row 2: With B, kfb, k to marker, rm, kfb, pm, k to last st, kfb—160 sts.

Rows 3 and 4: Repeat rows 1 and 2—168 sts.

Row 5: With A, kfbf, k to marker, rm, kfb, pm, k to last st, kfbf—173 sts.

Row 6: With A, kfb, p to marker, rm, pfb, pm, p to last st, kfb—176 sts.

Rows 7–10: Rep rows 5 and 6 twice—192 sts.

Rows 11–16: Rep rows 1 and 2 three times—216 sts.

Rows 17–22: Rep rows 5 and 6 three times—240 sts.

Rows 23–26: Rep rows 1 and 2 twice—256 sts.

Row 27: Rep row 1—261 sts.

Bind off loosely to marker, rm, k1, slip back to left needle, k1, bind off, then bind off to end.

Large Version Only

With RS facing and A, pick up 106 sts on first half of triangle, pick up 1 st at center point, place marker, and 106 sts on second half of triangle—213 sts total.

Set-up Row (WS): With A, kfb, p to marker, rm, pfb, pm, p to last st, kfb—216 sts.

Row 1: With A, kfbf, k to marker, rm, kfb, pm, k to last st, kfbf—221 sts.

Row 2: With A, kfb, p to marker, rm, pfb, pm, p to last st, kfb—224 sts.

Rows 3 and 4: Rep rows 1 and 2—232 sts.

Row 5: With B, kfbf, k to marker, rm, kfb, pm, k to last st, kfbf—235 sts.

Row 6: With B, kfb, k to marker, rm, kfb, pm, k to last st, kfb—238 sts.

Rows 7–10: Rep rows 5 and 6 twice—254 sts.

Rows 11–16: Rep rows 1 and 2 three times—278 sts.

Rows 17–20: Rep rows 5 and 6 twice—294 sts.

Row 21: Rep row 1—299 sts.

Bind off loosely to marker, rm, k1, slip back to left needle, k1, bind off, then bind off to end.

FINISHING

Weave in ends.

techniques

Here are the commonly used techniques in *One + One: Wraps, Cowls & Capelets*.

Casting On

LONG-TAIL CAST-ON

Leaving a tail long enough to cast on the required number of stitches (1 inch per stitch is plenty for all but the bulkiest of yarns), make a slipknot and place it on the needle. *Wrap the tail around your thumb and the working yarn around your index finger. Hold the yarn ends with your other three fingers (figure 1). Insert the needle into the loop around your thumb from front to back and over the yarn around your index finger (figures 2 and 3). Bring the needle down through the loop on your thumb (figure 4). Drop the loop off your thumb and tighten the stitch. Repeat from * for the required number of stitches.

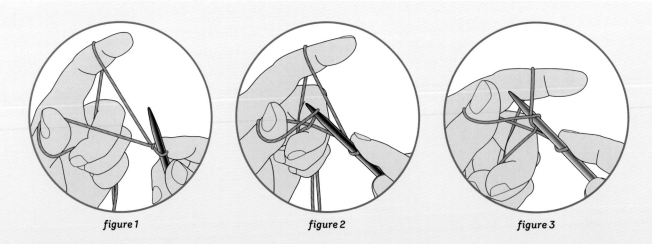

figure 1   *figure 2*   *figure 3*

KNITTED CAST-ON

This method can be used to begin a project, and it also allows you to add new stitches to stitches you've already knitted. If you don't have stitches on your needle yet, cast on one stitch by placing a slipknot on the needle, and hold the needle in your left hand. Insert the right needle into the first stitch on the left needle, as if to knit it. Knit the stitch, but don't drop the stitch from the left needle. Place the newly knitted stitch back on the left needle (figure 5). Continue adding new stitches in this manner until you have added as many stitches as the pattern calls for.

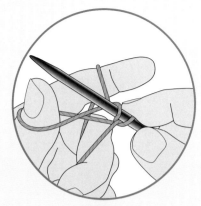

figure 4

PROVISIONAL CAST-ON, CROCHET VERSION

This method allows you to knit from both the top and bottom of each cast-on stitch. Once you've knitted a few rows, the stitches can be put back on needles and knitted in the other direction. A smooth, contrasting color of scrap yarn can easily be identified and undone to expose the live stitches.

Using a crochet hook and smooth scrap yarn, chain the number of stitches called for in the pattern, plus an additional five or so. On one side of the chain, the stitches form Vs, and on the other side of the chain, the stitches form bumps. Insert the knitting needle into the bump of the stitch next to the one forming the loop on the hook and knit it (figure 6). Continue along the chain, knitting into each following bump, until you have the number of stitches required by the pattern. Now attach the main knitting yarn and start to knit as instructed. After several rows of knitting, or when directed in the pattern, remove the scrap yarn and carefully transfer the live stitches at the bottom edge to a knitting needle. You'll now be able to work these stitches in the other direction.

figure 5

LONG TAIL PROVISIONAL CAST-ON

Make a slipknot with the working yarn and waste yarns held together and place it on the needle (slipknot does not count as the first stitch). Adjust working yarn and waste yarn so that waste yarn is draped over your thumb (in the front) and working yarn is draped over your forefinger (in the back). Work Long Tail Cast-On. After the next knitted row, slip the slipknot off the needle.

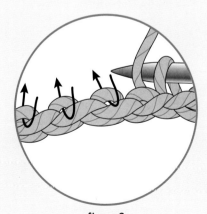

figure 6

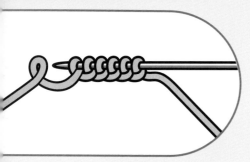

figure 7

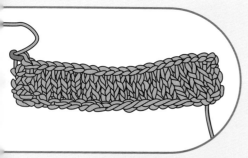

figure 8

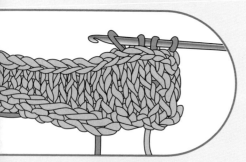

figure 9

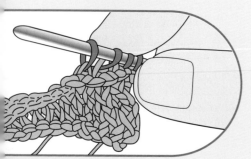

figure 10

BACKWARD-LOOP CAST-ON

*Loop working yarn and place it on needle backward so that it doesn't unwind. Repeat from *. (See figure 7.)

Picking Up Stitches

STANDARD METHODS

Some projects require that stitches be picked up from the bound-off (horizontal) or side (vertical) edge of a knitted piece. Work with the right side facing you. On the horizontal edge, insert the needle into the first stitch under the bound-off edge and pull a loop through; on the vertical edge, insert the needle between the running threads of the first two stitches and pull a loop through. Continue in this fashion as directed in the pattern.

WITH DECORATIVE EDGE SHOWING

Step 1: Bind off sts in color A as instructed (figure 8).

Step 2: Using a crochet hook and color B, with the right side facing, pick up and pull a loop through the back of the bind off chain leaving the bind off chain untouched and exposed (figures 9 and 10).

Step 3: Keep going across entire bind-off edge until all the required sts have been picked up, transferring the sts from the crochet hook to your needle when necessary to make more room on the crochet hook for picking up remaining stitches (figures 11 and 12).

Step 4: Once all the sts are picked up and transferred, follow instructions to continue with color B. You will see a decorative edge on the facing right side that has been formed where the stitches were picked up (figure 13).

Binding Off

There are many ways to bind off; here are several techniques used in the book.

LOOSE BIND-OFF

The easiest way to bind off loosely is by using larger needles. If these are not available, merely knit every other stitch twice before binding it off. Work as follows: *Knit one stitch. Knit a second stitch. Transfer the last stitch knitted back to the left-hand needle; knit it again. Bind it off by pulling the first stitch on the right-hand needle over it; repeat from *.

THREE-NEEDLE BIND-OFF

The three-needle bind-off is used to join two pieces together while binding off, eliminating the need to sew seams. With the right sides of the knitted fabric that you're joining facing each other, hold the two needles together in your left hand. With a third needle in your right hand, knit two stitches together, working one stitch from the front needle and one stitch from the back needle. *Knit the next two stitches together as before, taking one stitch from the front and one from the back. Pass the previous stitch worked over the latest stitch worked, to bind off. Repeat from * until all stitches have been bound off (figure 14).

STRETCHY BIND-OFF (JENY'S SURPRISINGLY ELASTIC BIND-OFF)

Yo (back to front), k1, insert LH needle into yo and pull it over k1. [*yo, k1, insert LH needle into yo and pull it over k1, BO right st over left st]. Rep bracketed instructions until 1 st remains. Cut yarn and pull through last st.

Assorted Techniques

WORKING IN THE ROUND

Most large-diameter projects are worked on circular needles in the round. Circular needles for cowls and capes are generally 16"–24"/40.5–61cm around at most. Use your favorite method to join in the round, being careful not to twist the stitches and making sure that your working yarn is not inside the circle of stitches. For a clean join you can cast on one extra stitch, then join to knit in the round by slipping the first cast-on stitch from left to right, and pass the slipped stitch over the extra cast-on stitch. It is good practice to place a marker to identify the start of a round. The only exception is in the Quilted Cowl, where you will be instructed to twist your work deliberately before joining to knit in the round.

When working small-diameter sections in the round, such as the Feather Poncho, the small number of stitches will no longer fit on circular needles. There are two options:

Double pointed needles (dpns) are commonly used: Place as close to the same amount of stitches on each of three or four double pointed needles. Knit around using a fourth or fifth double pointed needle. Pull tight to avoid gaps between stitches when switching from one needle to another.

Two circular needles are also used: Just as you would with circular knitting on double pointed needles, you need to distribute the stitches onto the two circular needles as evenly as possible. Work the needles on one end of the

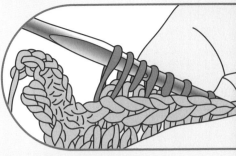

figure 11

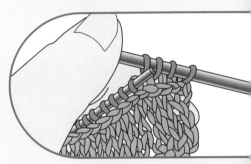

figure 12

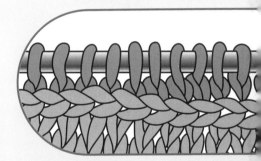

figure 13

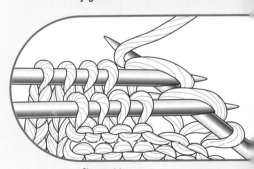

figure 14

figure 15

figure 16

figure 17

circular needle with the needle that is on the other end of that same circular needle. Once all the stitches on the first needle are knitted, continue knitting the stitches on the second needle in the same fashion. Slide them in the proper position to keep them in order. As before, pull tight to avoid gaps between stitches when switching from one needle to the other.

CARRYING YARNS

Here are two scenarios:

When one yarn is used for two rows, it is fairly simple to carry one yarn up along the side when working with the other. Not much thought needs to be given when the yarns alternate every other row.

When yarn is carried along for more than two rows, you will need to fasten the unworked yarn every two rows by twisting it from behind and around to the front of the working yarn. Otherwise the loopy edge will be unattractive and detract from the garment. Make sure not to pull too tightly or leave the yarn too loose. You will need to maintain good tension so that the piece will lie properly.

INTENTIONALLY UNRAVELING STITCHES

To unravel a stitch, simply slide it off your left-hand needle and gently tug on the yarn on either side of the loop until it creates a series of "rungs" of a ladder, going all the way down to the cast on row. This is used in the Elizabethan Collar to fan out the bottom of the collar.

SHORT ROWS WITH AND WITHOUT WRAPS

Edging short rows as in the Thick and Thin Wrap, the Old and New Shawl, the Vineyard Shawl, and the Feather Poncho do not require wraps, so little need be said except that it is important to follow the instructions exactly and never stop to take a break in the middle of a row. Always break only after you have knitted back and all your stitches are on one needle. These instructions will just use the word "Turn."

However, the Two-Color Sideways Garter Shawl uses short rows that are knitted using "Wrap and Turn" (w&t) in Garter Stitch. You will find that the instructions tell you to wrap and turn the short rows. Wrap short rows as follows:

When knitting in the pattern, when instructions say "wrap and turn," slip the next stitch purlwise, bring the yarn forward between the needles from the back to the front, slip the same stitch back to the left needle (figure 15), turn; the yarn will be in back ready to knit back.

When all the short rows are worked, smooth the transition between the extra rows and close up the holes from the turns by picking up the wrap along with its stitch on the return row.

Knit to the wrapped stitch. Insert the needle knitwise into the wrap and the stitch that was wrapped (figure 16); knit them together (figure 17), dropping the wrap to the other side of the work (figure 18).

FOLLOWING CHARTS IN KNITTING

Some patterns offer charts so that you can visually see how the pattern is formed, whether it is lace or colorwork. Follow each chart round by round (or row by row)—these are always numbered. Repeat the chart the number of times specified in the pattern. Use the key provided to identify what each symbol means. On the colorwork charts, different colors are used to distinguish color A from color B.

STRANDED KNITTING

When knitting using two colors, as in the Stranded Loop Cowl, one color will be used at a time and the other color will be carried in the back on the wrong side of the work. Make sure to carry the unused yarn loosely so that it does not pucker the fabric, but not too loosely so that it does not form unsightly loops.

Finishing Details and Decorative Elements

BLOCKING

Dampen the garment and lay it flat on a blocking board or rubber surface. Use T Pins to pin out decorative lace edging and points (where applicable). Make sure you use a measuring tape to ensure you are blocking garment to required dimensions. Let it dry flat before removing pins and moving the garment.

MAKING FRINGE

You'll make fringe for the Always the Right Time Striped Shawl. Using the number and length of strands specified in the project, hold the strands together evenly, folding them in half to make a loop. Insert a large crochet hook into the garment where you'll be applying the fringe and catch all the strands in the center.

Draw the loop end through (figure 19), making it large enough so you can pull the ends of the yarn through the loop (figure 20). Pull down on the ends so the loops tighten snugly around the stitch.

figure 18

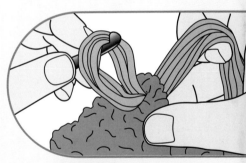

figure 19

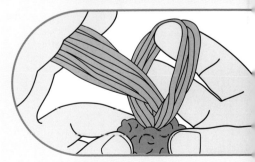

figure 20

Knitting Abbreviations

ABBR.	DESCRIPTION	ABBR.	DESCRIPTION	ABBR.	DESCRIPTION	ABBR.	DESCRIPTION
[]	work instructions within brackets as many times as directed	k2tog	knit 2 sts together – 1 st decreased	pm	place marker (first use spelled out)	sm	slip marker (first use spelled out)
()	work instructions within parentheses as many times as directed	k3tog	knit 3 sts together – 2 sts decreased	rm	remove marker (first use spelled out)	ssk	slip, slip, knit – 1 st decreased
**	repeat instructions following the asterisks as directed	kfb	knit in front and back of same st – 1 st increased	rep	repeat	sssk	slip, slip, slip, knit—2 sts decreased
*	repeat instructions following the single asterisk as directed	kfbf	knit in front, back, and front again of same st—2 sts increased	RH	right hand	st(s)	stitch(es)
"	inches	LH	left hand	RS	right side	tbl	through back loop(s)
BO	bind off	M1	make 1 – 1 st increased	rnd(s)	round(s)	tog	together
cdd	center double decrease – 2 sts decreased	M1L	make 1 left – 1 st increased	skp	slip, knit, pass slipped st over—1 st decreased	w&t	wrap and turn
CO	cast on	M1P	make 1 purl st – 1 st increased	sk2p	slip 1, knit 2 together, pass slipped st over—2 sts decreased	WS	wrong side
dec	decrease	p	purl	sl	slip	wyib	with yarn in back
inc	increase	pfb	purl in front and back of same st—1 st increased	sl1	slip 1	yo	yarn over
k	knit	p2tog	purl 2 sts together—1 st decreased	sl1p	slip 1 purlwise	yo2	yarn over twice

Yarn Weights

YARN WEIGHT SYMBOL & CATEGORY NAMES	0 lace	1 super fine	2 fine	3 light	4 medium	5 bulky	6 super bulky
TYPE OF YARNS IN CATEGORY	Fingering 10-count crochet thread	Sock, Fingering, Baby	Sport, Baby	DK, Light Worsted	Worsted, Afghan, Aran	Chunky, Craft, Rug	Bulky, Roving

Source: Craft Yarn Council of America's www.YarnStandards.com

Needle Size Chart

METRIC (MM)	US	UK/ CANADIAN
2.0	0	14
2.25	1	13
2.75	2	12
3.0	—	11
3.25	3	10
3.5	4	—
3.75	5	9
4.0	6	8
4.5	7	7
5.0	8	6
5.5	9	5
6.0	10	4
6.5	10½	3
7.0	—	2
7.5	—	1
8.0	11	0
9.0	13	00
10.0	15	000
12.0	17	—
16.0	19	—
19.0	35	—
25.0	50	—

Yarn Substitution Chart

YARN IN PROJECT	WEIGHT	YARN SUBSTITUTION
Artyarns Cashmere 1-ply	0	Filatura di Crosa Centolavaggi
Artyarns Beaded Silk & Sequins Light	3	S. Charles Crystal
Artyarns Ensemble Light	3	S. Charles Luna
Artyarns Silk Rhapsody Glitter Light	3	Filatura di Crosa Nirvana and Superior (held together)
Artyarns Ensemble Glitter Light	3	S. Charles Luna
TSCArtyarns Tranquility	3	Filatura di Crosa Nirvana and Superior (held together)
TSCArtyarns Tranquility Glitter	3	Filatura di Crosa Nirvana and Superior (held together)
Artyarns Ensemble 4	4	Tahki Mimosa
Artyarns Silk Essence	0	Filatura di Crosa Centolavaggi
TSCArtyarns Zara Hand-Dyed	3	Filatura di Crosa Zara
TSCArtyarns Cashmere Tweed	3	Filatura di Crosa Zara
TSCArtyarns Vanessa	4	S. Charles Tivoli
Artyarns Rhapsody Light	3	Filatura di Crosa Nirvana and Superior
Artyarns Beaded Ensemble and Sequins	4	S. Charles Tivoli
Artyarns Cashmere Glitter	3	S. Charles Ritratto
Artyarns Cashmere 5	4	S. Charles Jasmine
Artyarns Ultrabulky	5	Filatura di Crosa Zara 14
Artyarns Beaded Ensemble	4	S. Charles Tivoli
Artyarns Cashmere Sock Yarn	3	Filatura di Crosa Zarina
Artyarns Cashmere 3	3	Filatura di Crosa Zarina
Artyarns Beaded Pearl	4	Filatura di Crosa Stella
Artyarns Beaded Pearl & Sequins	4	Filatura di Crosa Stella
Artyarns Silk Mohair	0	Filatura di Crosa Superior
Artyarns Beaded Silk Light	3	S. Charles Crystal
Artyarns Cashmere 2	1	Filatura di Crosa Nirvana
Artyarns Silk Pearl	3	S. Charles Celine

About the Designers

TANYA ALPERT

Tanya Alpert is a Ukraine-born fiber artist, knitwear designer, and author of *Haiku Knits*. She graduated from the Kiev College of Applied Arts, Ukraine, and after moving to the United States in 1988, she worked as a graphic artist while designing and exhibiting her fiber art pieces around the country. In 2005, she opened her yarn boutique, Knitting by the Beach, in Solana Beach, California, where she began teaching and designing knitwear.

LISA ELLIS

Lisa Ellis is a knitwear designer and travelling knitting instructor in the greater Seattle/Tacoma area. Lisa is a contributing designer to over a dozen books and magazines and her patterns can be found in over one hundred yarns shops across the country as well as numerous online stores and catalogs. Her website is www.LisaEllisDesigns.com.

DEBORAH FRANK

Deborah Frank is self taught in knitting, crochet, and pattern design. She began writing knitting patterns in 2009. Under the name ObliviousKnits, she has created original lace shawl patterns using charts. Deborah's patterns can be found here: http://www.ravelry.com/designers/deborah-frank.

SAMANTHA GLENN

Samantha Glenn learned to knit while finding herself with a lot of free time in graduate school. She quickly realized knitting was more fun than environmental policy and now works as the head of marketing for Artyarns. She lives in New York City with her boyfriend and dog.

PAM GRUSHKIN

Pam Grushkin is a lifelong knitter who shares her passion for knitting and crochet through teaching and designing. Her designs have been published in *Vogue Knitting*, *Knitting Socks with Hand painted Yarn*, *One + One Hats*, *Crochet One-Skein Wonders*, Tahki Stacy Charles, and independently as Knits with a Twist. She lives in Connecticut where she blogs at www.stitchandchat.blogspot.com.

LISA HOFFMAN

Lisa Hoffman is a yarn artist living in New York City who has published patterns in *Vogue Knitting* magazine and in the books *Vogue Knitting on the Go! Bags Two* and *Vogue Knitting on the Go! Mittens & Gloves*. Fiber and color direct Lisa's designs, and all her creations are garments she herself would want to wear.

JUDITH RUDNICK KANE

Judith Rudnick Kane has an extensive art background, holding a BFA and an MA in painting from Hunter College. She worked as a studio artist for many years and her paintings have been exhibited widely; she has taught art, color theory, and knitting at all age and skill levels. Judith is the owner of Yarns for Your Soul in Manchester Center, Vermont.

BROOKE NICO

Brooke Nico is from St. Louis, Missouri, where she is co-owner of Kirkwood Knittery and a mother to three wonderful children. Her designs have been featured in *Vogue Knitting*, *Debbie Bliss Magazine*, and *Knitter's Magazine*, and she is the author of *Lovely Knitted Lace* (Lark, 2014).

NICHOLE REESE

Nichole Reese designs for her company, bluegirl knits, as well as other publications. She teaches classes at her LYS, Knot Another Hat in the beautiful Columbia River Gorge in Oregon, as well as other venues in the Pacific Northwest. Nichole is an accountant who loves applying her skills in math and efficiency to her designs. You can check out her designs and keep up with her blog at www.bluegirlknits.com.

SHARON SORKEN

Sharon Sorken has been a passionate knitter all her life, for pleasure and eventually for a livelihood. Her designs are sold in stores all over the country. Nancy Reagan appeared for a television interview in one of her designs.

HEATHER WALPOLE

Heather Walpole is the owner of Ewe Ewe Yarns. She has a background in design and created Wooly Worsted, a fine merino wool yarn with a great bounce and fresh color palette. She loves creating patterns that are fast to knit and fun to wear. She lives in California where she knits, cooks, and gardens with her husband and three crazy dogs. Check out her website at www.eweewe.com.

LYNN M. WILSON

Lynn M. Wilson is a designer, knitting instructor, and dedicated knitter. Lynn's designs have been featured in *Knit Simple Magazine*, *60 Quick Knits in Cascade 200*, *60 Quick Baby Knits*, and *Vogue Knitting on the Go! Bags Two*. She has designed for Be Sweet Yarns and Tanglewood Fiber Creations, and has her own collection of Lynn Wilson Designs knitting patterns. More information is available on her website: www.lwilsondesigns.com.

JENNIFER WOOD

Jennifer Wood designs for Wood House Knits. She taught herself to knit ten years ago and loved it so much she began designing her own patterns. It has been a wonderful outlet for her creative energy. She has an absolutely wonderful husband, three amazing children, a fine son-in-law, a sweet, sweet grandbaby, and two bad dogs. Her patterns can be found on her website, www.woodhouseknits.com, and at www.ravelry.com under woodhouseknits.

NELL ZIROLI

Nell Ziroli is a perpetual knitter, published designer, and enthusiastic teacher. She comes from a family of knitters and otherwise crafty people and has been creating things by hand for as long as she can remember. She also feels at home in the kitchen. Nell lives in Atlanta in a little house on a hill with her youngest daughter, Haley. You can read about her thoughts and work on her blog: www.knitnellknit.blogspot.com.

LAURA ZUKAITE

A native Lithuanian and a graduate from Parsons The New School for Design, Laura is happily pursuing her career as a sweater designer in New York City. She is the author of *Luxe Knits* (Lark Crafts, 2009) and *Luxe Knits: The Accessories* (Lark Crafts, 2010), books that feature designs made with exceptional yarns that convey Laura's design philosophy. Her website is www.laurazukaite.com.

Photo by: Elliot Schreier

About the Author

Iris Schreier couldn't find the yarn she wanted for her designs and, with the mission of elevating the art of knitting, decided to create it herself. She is the founder of Artyarns, a company that has built its reputation on producing luxurious, sophisticated, hand-dyed yarns of the highest quality. Since 2004, Artyarns has offered a variety of special yarns, including merino wool, silk, cashmere, and mohair, and has featured fiber blends as well as embellished yarns enhanced with beads, sequins, and gold or silver metallic strands.

Taught by her mother, Iris has been knitting since she was about six years old. She has always been drawn to decorative and fanciful types of projects and is known best for her unique designs for modular knitting, lacework, and reversible knitwear. Iris is the author of several Lark books, including *Exquisite*

Little Knits (with co-author Laurie Kimmelstiel, 2004), *Modular Knits* (2005), *Lacy Little Knits* (2007), *Iris Schreier's Reversible Knits* (2009), *One + One: Scarves, Shawls & Shrugs* (2012), *and One + One: Hats* (2012).

Her original techniques are used in knitting workshops around the world, and her patterns have been translated into various languages.

Iris has appeared on the television programs Knitty Gritty and Needle Arts Studio, and she has written articles and published patterns in leading magazines. Visit her Facebook page at http://www.facebook.com/artyarns and see her designs on her web-sites: http://www.artyarns.com/about-us/.

Acknowledgments

Without the support of the incredible group of designers who contributed to this collection, it would just not have been possible to create this book. You have totally outdone yourselves! Samantha Glenn wears two hats: She is one of the talented designers included in this book and also works at Artyarns—I could absolutely not have done it without you Sam; you pulled everything together. Thanks to Sue and Sheila who pitched in with last-minute test-knitting. And as always, Elliot and my boys Jason and Owen, and my knitting group buddies, Diane, Barbara, Lesley, Francy, and Monica, gave me incredible faith and encouragement to develop new designs. And my Facebook and Ravelry friends who participated in the knitalongs that brought about some interesting designs included here.

Many thanks to everyone at Lark who has pulled this together including Kay J. Hay (technical editor), Iris Bass (proofreader), Shannon Yokeley (art director), Orrin Lundgren (illustrator), Dawn Dillingham (editorial assistant), and Lynne Harty (photographer), as well as Amanda Carestio who helped me come up with the concept of the third book of the series and provided editorial oversight throughout. And a special thanks to my editor, Shannon Quinn-Tucker!

Editors: Shannon Quinn-Tucker and Amanda Carestio
Art Director: Shannon Yokeley
Illustrator: Orrin Lundgren
Photography: Lynne Harty
Cover Designer: Igor Satanovsky

Project index